Salt in a Secular Society

How to make a difference now

Jacki Thomas

Acknowledgements

My thanks to:

The Hospice Chaplains
who willingly gave their time to be interviewed.

Prof Peter Tyler and Dr Lynne Scholefield of St Mary's University,
Twickenham, supervisors for my doctorate.

My good friend Janet who read my script and made many helpful
and practical suggestions.

Fiona for proof-reading with an auditor's eye.

Gill for the cover sketch and Carolyn for her graphic artist skills.

The Revd. Nigel Richards, Vicar of All Saints Dedworth,
for his encouragement.

My husband Mike,
without whom this book would not have been written.

Contents

Preface

Speaking on evangelism in May 2016, Archbishop Justin Welby commended to fellow Christians the approach of respecting the other, listening before speaking and not speaking about faith unless asked. The Archbishop might have been describing the approach of a hospice chaplain who is prohibited from preaching the Gospel but may speak about faith if asked and nevertheless symbolizes God's presence. My doctoral research with hospice chaplains explored and analysed the chaplain's role of providing spiritual care. Such care is understood as recognizing and responding to the needs of the human spirit which flourishes when there is meaning and purpose to life. Recognizing support systems and sources of strength and comfort, giving and receiving love, coping with pain, fear, loss, loneliness, being able to tell one's story and be listened to are all aspects of spiritual care. It is important to note that spiritual care may or may not include a faith or belief system and may or may not include God.

In other words, the chaplain keeps his/her job by acknowledging and adapting to the predominantly secular environment of the hospice. It is my belief that the experience of the hospice chaplain is not only relevant to the world outside the hospice but has much to offer to equip God's people to be the salt of the earth. When I presented some of my research with hospice chaplains, together with some of my own experiences from fourteen years of hospice chaplaincy and twenty-five years of Spiritual Direction, at the Conference of Licensed Lay Ministers in the Oxford Diocese the ministers asked when the material would be available in a book. This is the result of that request.

Jacki Thomas
November 2019

Subsequent to writing the original Preface the Coronavirus has struck and anxiety, fear and panic have become prevalent in our society. With isolation, loneliness and loss increasing daily it is imperative that we know who we are in Christ, recognizing our sources of strength and comfort in order to help others find their sources of strength and comfort. We all need to feel part of our community, to be able to speak and know that we are listened to, to know that we matter. Never has there been a greater need for salt in our society than now.

Jacki Thomas
April 2020

Introduction

Salt in a secular society...

'You are the salt of the earth; but if salt has lost its taste, how can its saltiness be restored? It is no longer good for anything, but is thrown out and trampled under foot.' (NRSVA Matthew 5: 13)

'Let me tell you why you are here. You're here to be salt-seasoning that brings out the God-flavors of this earth. If you lose your saltiness, how will people taste Godliness? You've lost your usefulness and will end up in the garbage.' (The Message Matthew 5: 13)

Jesus is telling his followers that they, and we, need to be salt. What does he mean? Let's consider the role of salt in relation to food: salt preserves, enabling food to be stored; when food is cooked it is salt that brings out its flavour. Jesus is telling his followers that as salt we are the means by which God's creation does not die or disintegrate but lives and flourishes. We are the means by which God's creation, including humanity, is cared for. I use 'we' because Jesus's instruction is not only addressed to those whom he has appointed 'apostles, prophets, evangelists, pastors and teachers' (Ephesians 4:11) but to all of us. Jesus wants us all to bring out God's flavour in his creation, he wants us all to point to God's presence in the world. Jesus wants each and every one of us to play our part in caring for and bringing fullness of life to all creation. The question is 'How?'

In this book I am offering some possible answers to this question, with examples taken from experience. It is my hope that my suggestions will stimulate thinking and ultimately, as Paul says, 'equip his people for works of service, so that the body of Christ may be built up...' (Ephesians 4:12).

At time of writing the persecution of Christians in various parts of the world is increasing. In our own country the voices of strident secularists are getting stronger, the place of religion is being defined or limited and the practice of the Christian faith is met with bewilderment and disdain. Many of the population say they are not religious but some describe themselves as 'spiritual' and others recognize that they have spiritual issues and needs. Still others, given the opportunity, might acknowledge their capacity for awe and wonder, say that they were missing something in life or observe 'there has to be more than this'. My understanding of the spiritual or spirituality is that it is the essence of being human. It is, to quote some of my chaplaincy colleagues, what 'floats my boat', 'what makes me tick', 'what makes me me and you you.' When there is meaning and purpose to life I flourish. I find such meaning and purpose in relationships, activities and the natural world. These are the source of the salt which I need to live and to flourish. Recognizing my salt I am then able to encourage others to find the salt in their lives – whether or not they have a faith or belief system, whether or not they believe in God. The important thing is that I believe that this is how God nourishes me and helping others recognize how they are spiritually nourished is one way of being salt for the preservation of humanity.

Reflecting on my experience in lay ministry, spiritual direction, hospice chaplaincy and doctoral research, I observed two developments which have influenced my thinking about how Christians are to be salt in a secular society. One is the change in the way we form our individual identity and the other is the changing nature of care. In both areas Christianity and the Church have played significant roles. For centuries

Christianity was what the academics call 'the dominant discourse' in our society. This term indicates the source of power and control in decision-making in society. It determined behaviour and shaped the way individuals saw themselves and understood who they were. Today the development of identity is influenced by external expectations, rarely consciously acknowledged as rooted in faith, and often stemming from advertising and social media. Christianity also determined society's attitude and response to problems such as the treatment of the poor, the homeless, the sick, thus defining the concept of care. Down the centuries that influence declined and the nature and extent of care for the sick, and the attitude to the poor and the homeless changed. The exploration of these two areas provides the backdrop for examining the gifts and skills that may help Christians to be salt in a secular society but first...

Notes to the reader

On salt

Salt – chemical name sodium chloride – is found throughout creation, in the earth, the sea, plants and animals. It is an essential nutrient for the human body but is something that the body cannot produce itself. Salt plays a vital role in the regulation of many bodily functions and is contained in body fluids that transport oxygen and nutrients. It is also essential in maintaining the body's overall fluid balance. Salt, sodium chloride, enables the transmission of nerve impulses around the body. It regulates the electrical charges moving in and out of the cells in the body. It controls taste, smell and tactile processes. The presence of sodium ions is essential for the contraction of muscles, including that largest and most important muscle, the heart. It is fundamental to the operation of signals to and from the brain. Without sufficient sodium your senses would be dulled, your nerves would not function, and from personal experience blood pressure drops.

Applying this description of salt to ourselves as Christians:

We, 'the salt of the earth' also known as disciples of Christ, are an essential nutrient for all creation, the earth and humanity. We cannot become salt by ourselves, nor can we be made salt by any other aspect of creation. We play a vital role in the regulation of activities which are society's bodily functions. We are to be found in all walks of life.

Our presence is essential for organisations to work properly and fairly, and be accountable for their business practices and their treatment of employees.

Our presence is essential to ensure that society's attitudes to all people, including the poor, the disadvantaged, the sick, the unemployed, the homeless, refugees, prisoners, are influenced and guided by justice and mercy expressed in loving care and concern.

Our presence is essential to ensure that society's attitudes to our environment in creation are not dulled by greed, expediency or apathy.

In short we Christians are essential for the maintenance of a balanced, just and fair society – where we are missing, low in numbers or have little influence a culture of entitlement and even impunity may develop and society become lawless.

My hope is that Christians will not only explore how they can be salt but realize that our society needs the salt of Christianity.

How to use this book

I hope that you will not try to read this book in one sitting but take time to reflect on the ideas. To help your reflection each chapter ends with a section entitled *Food for thought* which contains questions to stimulate your thinking. If others are also reading the book these questions may form the basis of a discussion group.

Chapter One

Just how salty have we been?

Introduction

From medieval times through to the Second World War Christianity and Christian values dominated our society. Academics referred to it as the 'dominant discourse' meaning that institutional Christianity, in the form of the established church, provided society's moral compass. After the Second World War institutional Christianity was still the source for defining right and wrong, the source for attitudes to and treatment of the poor and the sick. Whether this Christian dominant discourse was the equivalent of the salt to which Jesus refers is debateable. On the one hand Christianity fulfilled the role of salt, ensuring that attitudes to and care of the poor and sick were influenced and guided by justice and mercy. On the other hand Christianity was the source for the hierarchical structure of society which maintained and preserved the status quo, controlling behaviour and restricting social mobility, such that only part of society flourished. We might compare this with salting only part of a dish or some of the vegetables.

In medieval times the established church was Roman Catholic and post-reformation the official established church was the Church of England. However, looking back on my childhood I can see that adults of various denominations, including Methodists and Brethren, were as keen to maintain the status quo as those in the Church of England. I am going to use the term institutional Christianity in order to encompass other Christian churches, cults and movements as well as the Church of England. As part of established society institutional Christianity was a major influence on how people developed individual identity until the latter part of the twentieth century. Although that influence has declined it is part of our recent history. It is therefore helpful to consider how that history, including Evangelicalism, has contributed to the development of individual identity today. Understanding such external expectations may help us assess whether that sense of identity equips us to be salt.

What might we have inherited? Evangelicalism as salt?
To consider the extent to which history contributes to our sense of who we are we begin in the eighteenth and nineteenth century when the practice of religion was expressed through conformity and submission to authority. Victorian congregations conformed and submitted to the power of the established churches. Evangelicalism, an interdenominational movement dedicated to spreading the Gospel, challenged this power.

Although it has changed over time Evangelicalism has always had and still has four common features referred to as the Bebbington quadrilateral. David Bebbington, a historian generally recognized as the authority on Evangelicalism, identified the four characteristics as: devotion to the Bible, belief in the necessity of Christ's sacrifice on the cross, a belief in the necessity of conversion, and the need to actively spread the good news of the gospel[1].

If you are thinking that surely these are true of all Christians you are probably right but Evangelicals do not share the High Churchman's belief in the role of the priest as mediator of the grace of God to the people, nor do they believe in the Real Presence of Christ in the Sacrament. Rather Evangelicals believe in the priesthood of all believers and that the communion is a memorial act, shared in remembrance of Jesus.

Nineteenth century Evangelicalism challenged the established churches by focusing on what we today might describe as the subservience of the lower classes, that is anyone who was not upper class. Cultural historian Callum Brown shows how Evangelicalism offered a way of life for the middle and working classes, giving them the opportunity to participate in the congregation and in society[2].

Evangelical congregations developed their own moral authority to which members submitted rather than submitting to external authority, making religion a matter of personal salvation rather than submission to ecclesial authority. Such salvation was expressed in actively spreading the gospel and from 1796 to 1914 the tenets of Evangelicalism seeped into British society:

> The hundred years or so before the First World War nevertheless deserve to be called the Evangelical century. In the period the activism of the movement enabled it to permeate British society.[3]

Evangelicalism was thus like salt seeping into food. Unfortunately the evangelical salt did not reach everyone. True it was inter-denominational but it was led by men for whom it provided a strong sense of duty. Fulfilling that duty contributed to a sense of identity. Women on the other hand were expected to be submissive, so they fulfilled their duty by choosing the home rather than the world. It seems that they believed that through them their husbands and children were saved. Despite their submission and the emphasis on the domestic role it was the women who fulfilled the duty of care, making pastoral visits and campaigning on behalf of the poor and the destitute. It would appear that, although they had not benefitted from the evangelical salt, women were themselves the salt that provided the moral conscience of Victorian society and the means by which the lower orders were cared for and controlled. Thus Evangelicalism was a movement led by men but practised, in the sense of actively demonstrating and spreading the salty gospel, by women.

The decline of the power of external expectations

In the nineteenth century unwritten but socially recognized rules governed behaviour such that everyone constructed their identity following what was expected of them. These external expectations were anchored in the Christian faith, as taught by the Churches, and therefore derived their authority from God. Subjective or interior experiences were deemed irrelevant at best and wrong at worst. External expectations appear to have caused many young men to join up to defend their country in the First World War. The fact that many of these young men died caused a general questioning of faith, further challenged by the Depression of the 1930s, casting serious doubt on the power and authority of God and the Church, especially the Church of England. Consequently the foundation of the external expectations was suspect and personal identity had lost its clearly identifiable underpinnings. It seems that this expression of institutional Christianity has failed to bring out the flavour of God's creation.

In addition the 1920s saw the break down of the inter-denominational unity of Evangelicalism and its strength weakened. The transmission of the Christian beliefs, passed from generation to generation, mainly by women, also waned. Consequently the sense of identity and security found in personal redemption in the nineteenth century was gradually lost in the twentieth century. If Evangelicalism was like salt in society it had now lost its flavour. Faith and conversion to Christianity were not valued, were not even talked about, and the need to conform reasserted itself. The effects of the First World War and the Depression meant that security was initially about survival. Having survived those major events the individual's concern with faith and salvation was superseded by the attraction of leisure pursuits such as cinemas, pubs, gambling, the wireless and the availability of tobacco and alcohol. Perhaps relief at having survived gave way to hedonism – albeit hedonism within establishment boundaries. Salt was no longer valued nor thought relevant.

Nevertheless institutional Christianity in the establishment continued to assert itself. Events such as the abdication of Edward as king were seen by the establishment as potentially de-stabilizing. The press barons (Northcliffe, Rothermere, Beaverbrook) were part of the establishment and played their part in ensuring that details did not appear in the press. If you have seen the film 'The King's Speech' you may recall that Archbishop Lang, played by Derek Jacobi, was astonished that the future King George VI had chosen a speech therapist without consulting him. Furthermore the Archbishop felt it only right that he should recommend someone. This scene may be stretching things a little but it indicates the nature of the role the Church of England played or thought it should play.

In contrast the Second World War gives us an example of the cohesive role which was played by institutional Christianity. People from all walks of life and levels of society, with but mostly without commitment to Jesus Christ, were willing to accept governmental (establishment) control because they were united against a common enemy. However, once the war was over the need for the cohesion disappeared. People remembered the pre-war years in which the establishment, including institutional Christianity, had done little to ease deteriorating housing conditions and unemployment, poverty and ill-health were common. Consequently there was a paradigm shift in the attitude of the population to the establishment, which to most people was synonymous with both the Conservative Party and the Church of England, such that the Labour Party won a landslide victory in the 1945 election. The salty role of institutional Christianity had failed to serve its purpose.

My father was a staunch member of the Labour party who was delighted with the election result. He subsequently served the community as a Labour councillor, determined that mistakes would not be repeated. Unfortunately the reality was that one kind of establishment was replaced by another – still made up of white men who thought they knew what was best for everyone! Although she supported my father my mother had the wisdom to see this at the time, but her words fell on deaf ears and my father said she was 'ahead of her time'.

The demise of the establishment and the failure of the salt of Christianity was reinforced in the 1945 report *Towards the Conversion of England*. The report focused on equipping the Church of England for its task of converting the English people but observed:

> The really daunting feature of modern evangelism is not the masses of the population to be converted, but that most of the worshipping community are only half-converted[4].

Not only does this report question the saltiness of the worshippers but when Archbishop Temple, who was the inspiration behind the report, died in 1944 his replacement Geoffrey Fisher did not prioritise evangelism and the saltiness of the worshippers was irrelevant.

Curiously, although the Christian beliefs were no longer as obvious as they had been when Evangelicalism held sway, the effects of those beliefs were still in evidence. The experience of a friend illustrates the point: in the 1950s as a new manager he moved to a village near his factory in the north of England. Being committed Christians he and his wife went to morning service. His wife told him that the looks they were getting made her uncomfortable. As they left the church a man fell into step beside them and in a quiet voice said 'Management comes to Evening Prayer. Morning service is for the workers.' In small villages church attendance was still expected at that time. In urban areas such expectations were disappearing – in a street of one hundred and fifty houses my family was one of only a handful that went to church. Activities on Sundays were still restricted – by law in the case of shop opening hours and through habit in the case of hanging out washing – but in some areas walking to church was not a time of preparation for worship but rather an opportunity for a fashion parade for the girls and women. Using the salt analogy we might say that some effects of past usage, such as conformity, are preserved but the saltiness needed to bring out the flavour of flourishing seems to be fading.

Those of us who lived through the 1950s may remember that most families still honoured Victorian values of honesty, kindness and doing the 'right thing' and the young honoured their parents who had suffered the war for their freedom, but the evangelical beliefs were not taking root as they once had. The value of the effect of salt was appreciated but continued usage was not. The attempt to reawaken the evangelical need for personal salvation, and identity grounded in that salvation, was challenged by the advent of the bohemian and rebel lifestyles, the latter expressed in skiffle music and rock-and-roll. Awareness of these lifestyles gave an alternative source of identity which therefore no longer rested on being like one's parents. That awareness was facilitated by the changing nature of the mass media which from 1955 included ITV as well as BBC, and newspapers which were no longer solely owned by the pre-war oligarchy. Through the media liberal Christians were seen leading CND and anti-apartheid rallies, suggesting that the face of institutional Christianity was changing.

In 1960 Bishop Robinson appeared for Penguin in the Lady Chatterley Trial. This highlighted the Anglican Church's split over moral theology which up to that point had shored up society's 'ritual codes' which had been loosely based on Christian teaching. Society's moral values were further challenged by Conservative government scandals such as the Profumo affair which commanded a great deal of media attention in 1961. The early 1960s also included Vatican II, with its emphasis on liturgical reform, and a burst of evangelical Charismatic renewal. Until this point the Church of England was regarded as part of 'the establishment', along with the judiciary, the state, the landed classes and the press. Furthermore those who were 'religious' were identified with the establishment which was seen as restrictive and authoritarian. Against this backdrop there appeared satirical programmes like 'Beyond the Fringe' in 1960 and 'That Was the Week That Was' in 1962–3. These programmes used humour, irony, exaggeration and ridicule to expose and criticize wrong-doing and stupidity in politics, corporations and society generally. Their content could be seen as anti-establishment, epitomizing a rejection of control by church and authority figures such as parents, suggesting that they were anti-institutional Christianity.

Christianity and identity

Cultural historian Callum Brown says that until the 1960s Christianity 'infused public culture and was adopted by individuals, whether churchgoers or not, in forming their own identities'.[5] He even argues that the specific year of 1963 was the point at which Christianity lost its influence, but it is sufficient to say that the way any individual constructed his life and formed his identity changed in the 1960s. No longer did the socially accepted rules based on Christianity hold sway. In other words Christianity, as conveyed by the established church, maintained the status quo of 'the establishment' until the 1960s. Ironically the Church of England was itself part of the establishment. This is not to say that the Christian faith collapsed but that cultural or institutional Christianity collapsed. As salt this Christianity was no longer effective or even active in preserving and caring for God's creation. No longer was it seen as the recipe for human flourishing. Rather the narrative of institutional Christianity no longer stood alone but was joined by many other narratives – feminist, gay, liberationist, green, New Age – some of which still conveyed the unacknowledged saltiness of Christian values, as well as espousing a spiritual basis.

Summary

It appears that nineteenth century Evangelicalism fulfilled a salt-like role in that it challenged institutional Christianity's attitudes to and treatment of the lower classes, the poor and the sick. External expectations, rooted in institutional Christianity, maintained the structure and decorum of society until challenged by circumstances, such as the First World War and the Great Depression which changed the focus to the need for survival. An increased range of leisure pursuits then outweighed the attractions of personal salvation until the Second World War when the cohesive values of institutional Christianity came to the fore once more. After the Second World War institutional Christianity again lost influence and hierarchical, paternalistic authority was gradually replaced by the authority of the self. Gradually, therefore, the external expectations rooted in institutional Christianity lost their power and the self was no longer constrained in forming an identity.

1 Bebbington, D. (1989) *Evangelicalism in Modern Britain*, London: Routledge: 3

2 Brown, C. (2009) *The Death of Christian Britain*, (2nd ed), London: Routledge: 39.

3 Bebbington, D. (1989) *Evangelicalism in Modern Britain*, London: Routledge: 149.

4 Richardson, J. (2011) 'Anglican Evangelical Junior Clergy Conference Report', *Cross+Way* No. 122.

5 Brown, C. (2009) *The Death of Christian Britain*, (2nd ed), London: Routledge: 8.

Food for thought
- *To what extent did institutional Christianity fulfil the role of salt as referred to by Jesus?*
- *Is institutional Christianity so much a part of society that it too needs salt to preserve it and bring out its true flavour?*
- *What external expectations operate today?*
- *Consider the external expectations that influenced the formation of your identity.*
- *Identify Christian influences found in attitudes and decision-making today.*

Chapter two

'C of E' or 'spiritual but not religious'?

Please note: If you are not 'C of E' but a member of another church or religious group please do not think that this chapter is not for you. The term 'C of E' refers to the standard, one might say default, answer to the question 'what is your religion' on the societal attitude survey conducted from 2013 to 2015, as explained in this chapter.

Introduction

Just as our physical bodies struggle to function properly when our salt levels are low so our society struggles to maintain a balanced, just and fair ethos when the presence of Christian salt is low.

Until the twentieth century institutional Christianity played a crucial role in maintaining our society and contributed significantly to the development of individual identity. However, during the twentieth century that influence declined and the role of the Church of England in particular diminished. As the relevance of formal religion, in the Christianity taught by the churches, was challenged so the salt level in society was dropping. However, at the same time the appreciation of the relevance and awareness of spirituality or being spiritual was increasing. This chapter considers our understanding of spirituality, what we may have inherited, how it has changed, and its connection with Christian salt.

What might we have inherited? Awareness of 'the spiritual'

In medieval times 'the spiritual' or spirituality was inextricably linked with theology, specifically Christian theology and they were to be found together in the monastery. Theology was regarded as the articulation of spirituality and spirituality was seen as lived theology. The early development of healthcare shows Christian spirituality or lived theology in both the provision and the receipt of care of the sick, the poor and travellers. The pious gave alms to provide care and the recipients were morally obliged to pray for their benefactors[1].

No doubt the provision of this care was prompted by Jesus's words 'I needed clothes and you clothed me, I was sick and you looked after me, I was in prison and you came to visit me. ... Truly I tell you, whatever you did for one of the least of these brothers and sisters of mine, you did for me.' (Matthew 25:35...40). However, there is evidence that a stronger motivating factor was the desire to demonstrate one's piety in order to ease one's path through purgatory![2] Using the salt analogy it appears that the presence of Christian salt in medieval society was not entirely altruistic.

From the thirteenth century theology became more academic as it moved from monastery to university. By the nineteenth century it was a 'highly scholastic discipline'[3] whereas spirituality was still about the practice of piety. Using the analogy this would be like the study of salt as a chemical and the practical application of salt. The practice of spirituality or piety sometimes meant following prescriptive principles on how to pray – of which the church approved as it led the faithful to uniform perfection. Even today some people seem to think that chaplains visit to check that they are saying their prayers! The term spirituality was also used to refer to mystical prayer[4] – of which the church did not always approve! And if we are honest we will admit that there are times when the church still struggles with mystical prayer today.

Then in the 1970s and 1980s a new academic discipline, 'spirituality', emerged. It was no longer attached to theology or religion and had begun to appear in a variety of academic and professional disciplines outside traditional religion. In the 1970s the nursing profession were the first to use spirituality with this broader and apparently secular understanding as they responded to the need to provide spiritual, as well as medical and social, care for patients[5]. By analogy the practical application of salt is itself being studied and analysed. The academic reasons for spirituality's emergence, detached from its original mooring in the Christian faith, included a developing interest in eastern spirituality amongst certain sections of society and a general increase in 'the search for meaning, transcendence, personal integration and social transformation'[6]. In short: the search for meaning was no longer confined to the church.

Might another reason for the emergence of this spirituality, uncontrolled by the church, be the work of the Holy Spirit? Augustine[7] wrote 'You have made us for yourself, and our hearts are restless, until they can find rest in you.' Just as the physical body needs salt/sodium chloride so the spiritual body needs the salt of the Holy Spirit. Lest this sound as though the spiritual plays second fiddle to the physical let me make it clear that I believe that we are spiritual beings having a physical experience – not physical beings having a spiritual experience.

Also in the 1970s Alister Hardy, who had founded the Religious Experience Research Unit in Oxford in 1969, was exploring the nature of spiritual awareness in biological terms pointing to its important function of enabling individuals to survive. Alister Hardy was followed in 1985 by David Hay who was a zoologist and a pioneering researcher into the study of contemporary reports of spiritual and religious experience. He argued that spirituality is a natural awareness, a primordial human experience, a bodily awareness or 'felt sense' that is there before words or thinking[8]. Hay did not accept that human beings are born as atheists who are socialised into acquiring religious beliefs but the opposite, born with a vivid awareness of a transcendent dimension to life, born with a vivid awareness of salty spirituality which is gradually ignored or buried[9]. In simple terms: we are born as salty spiritual beings but as we grow we let our spiritual nature, our salt, be washed out of us!

As a result of his research Hay held that the loss of spiritual awareness was due to socialization and he was particularly critical of the role education plays in depriving children of their spiritual birthright[10]. I illustrate this loss with the story of a little girl, aged about five, who was excited to be in the garden on the first warm day of the year. She danced after a butterfly, crying 'look Daddy, a butterfly!' to which her father replied 'yes dear, but can you spell it?' The next few days were spent learning to spell butterfly. On the first warm day of the following year they went into the garden. The father said 'look dear, a butterfly'. The little girl spelt out 'b-u-t-t-e-r-f-l-y' but did not even glance at it. Of course children have to learn to spell but they also need to appreciate what the word they are spelling represents – they need the salt which gives balance in their education. The introduction of forest schools where children learn about plants and insects is beginning to bring balance – watch the excitement of a Year 1 class discovering worms and other creepy-crawlies!

Spirituality and spiritual care in practice
Detached from its original mooring in the Christian religion the concept of spirituality and the idea of 'being spiritual' joined the zeitgeist[11]. However, what the general public understood by either term was and still is varied, ranging from monasticism to wind chimes. Those charged with the provision of spiritual care, such as chaplains and nurses, were more likely to understand it as a process of transformation and growth.

As a hospice chaplain it was important for me to be able to explain 'spiritual care' to patients and staff. There were various official definitions available but like many hospice chaplains I felt that expressions like 'transcendent meaning and aspiration' were fine in the academic world but did little to express the actual experience of the patient or staff member. Similarly the use of the name sodium chloride is fine for academics but it does not describe its effect on food. Likewise for most healthy people a question about transcendent meaning is likely to be met with bewilderment. It is more likely that asking the person to talk about what mattered to them, what fed them when they were down, what gave them strength, where they found love, would help them understand their own spirituality. A colleague gave the example of a patient who was pining for her dog, saying that if the dog was her support and source of affection then let the dog visit....

One of my patients was an eighty-year-old lady who thought she was in for respite care but the family wanted her to stay to die in the hospice. She was miserable and determined to go home. I asked what she was missing. She told me that her eight-year-old grand-daughter would visit her everyday on the way home from school and dance for her. As she spoke her whole demeanour changed – she came to life. I asked whether the little girl was coming in to the hospice. The answer was that her parents would not let her as it was 'not a suitable place' for children. I would not have expected that lady to say that her granddaughter was the source of her spiritual nourishment but I believe that was the case and I was not surprised to find, a week later, that the lady had returned home to die. More down to earth ways of describing spiritual nourishment might be 'what floats your boat', 'what makes you who you are', 'what makes you tick', 'your engine', 'what makes me me and you you'. These expressions are more readily understood and help us to see that spirituality is at the core of our being. Furthermore, we see that spirituality is our sense of purpose, self-worth, significance and security and may or may not involve religion or God. Understanding spirituality in this way it is easy to see why some people describe themselves as 'spiritual but not religious', they have recognized the need for salt but without the trappings of the church. Equally, understanding spirituality in this way may give us an opening for helping the other person to explore their awareness of God – although they may not use the word God or may say that they believe 'there is something' rather than 'God'.

One Sunday morning I was giving the talk in a Baptism service. The majority of the congregation were not regular church-goers (they were dressed in their best clothes!). I asked them to name their favourite spiritual food. I was met with puzzled looks, so I told them to name their favourite physical food. That was easy – McDonald's and pizza were the responses. I returned to the spiritual food by using the overhead to show pictures of the night sky, waterfalls, a whale breaching, a new-born baby. The puzzled looks were replaced with expressions of at least thoughtfulness if not understanding.

Spiritual but not religious

Previously we saw how the decline in compliance with external expectations affected identity development. This decline is supported by research conducted from 2013 to 2015 by Linda Woodhead (Professor of the Sociology of Religion), in conjunction with YouGov. I attended a presentation by Professor Woodhead on the findings of this survey[12]. Starting in 2013 a baseline of 37% of the population stated that they had no religion. By February 2015 the figure was 42% and by December 2015 it was 46%[13]. Prior to this research previous societal attitude surveys showed the default position, the most common answer, when asked about religion was 'Church of England'. This was the expected, respectable and acceptable answer. However, the later research shows a marked decline in this category and an increase in those saying 'no religion', suggesting not only the rejection of hierarchy but also the rejection of membership or even identification with a distinct group, religious or secular. In particular the need to state that you were 'C of E' was losing ground. However, the survey found that the influence of secularism was minimal and only one quarter of those interviewed were confident that there is no God. Even although they said they had 'no religion' 25% claimed spiritual practices such as praying and 11% said they were spiritual. Answering a question from the floor Professor Woodhead interpreted the data to indicate that the 'nones', as she called them, are not hostile to religion. Nor does 'no religion' mean no spirituality and it does not impair the forging of identity.

The reaction of the hospice chaplain to those who describe themselves as 'spiritual but not religious' is the same as to those with a particular faith and those with no expressed faith: to be alongside and encourage the person to recognize their spirituality however they understand it and to identify their spiritual resources. One gentleman stated that his religion was the local rugby club and he really needed to see a game. For another young man, in his twenties, the only thing that mattered to him was football. He had never been to see his team play a match but wanted to do so before he died. The volunteer who had driven him to appointments had chatted with him and understood what it meant to him so arranged to take him to a match. 'What if he dies on the terraces?' cried the Nursing Manager. The answer was: 'He couldn't die in a better place'. The volunteer driver was a practising Christian and a football fan who appreciated the spiritual role that football played in that young man's life. So they went to the match – and the team lost!

The turn to the self

The turn away from external expectations to an internal authority – whether this be self, God or other – is true for many narratives, including the Christian. For Christians this subjective turn, referred to as the turn to the self, moves from the keeping of the Ten Commandments (Exodus 20:1-17) demonstrated in obedience to a way of life commanded by an external, transcendent source of authority, to the individual's subjective response to 'God so loved the world that he sent his only Son' (John 3:16). It is interesting that some academics associated this Christian subjective turn with the mystical tradition and therefore not relevant to their research!

In the Sermon on the Mount (Matthew 5), Jesus explained that conforming to the commandments such as 'you shall not murder', 'you shall not commit adultery' is not sufficient, but inner thoughts and feelings are just as wrong or unhealthy as the actual action. The person who angrily thinks 'I could murder him' has failed to keep the commandment 'do not murder' as much as the person who has committed murder. The person who looks lustfully at another has failed to keep the commandment 'do not commit adultery' just as much as the person who has committed adultery. Jesus points to an inward turn of self-awareness necessary for the keeping of The Commandments, a turn which recognizes that it is the relationship with God that enables the keeping. To be able to keep The Commandments the authority has to come from within, from the absorption of the laws into heart and mind (Hebrews 8:10), from the self-in-relation with God or, to put it another way, from the in-dwelling of Christ as expounded by Jesus in chapters 14 and 15 of John's gospel. This subjective life has rejected the hierarchy and deference of institutional Christianity and recognized the authority of the God who dwells within. Just as the salt does not sit on the surface but is absorbed into the casserole the Christian absorbs the salt of God the Holy Spirit.

Growing up in the 1950s and 1960s, my own experience of identity development was of external expectations mediated by a passionate Methodist minister who did a very good 'hell fire and brimstone' sermon, thus making a profound impression. Perhaps it is not surprising that it took me some fifteen years to realize that the external divine authority who was to be feared and obeyed was a misrepresentation and the internal divine authority who loved me actually longed for me to respond with love, thus forming a relationship. Like the salt in the casserole the relationship is not visible but the effects, the results, are seen in the flavour of life.

Summary

From the 1960s onwards the tacit recognition of authority in teachers, doctors, and the vicar, who might be described as experts in their respective fields, was replaced by the authority of the self, a self which no longer required membership of a group to attain identity. Where once the answer in societal attitude surveys had to be Church of England today's answer is 'none'. These 'nones', who have no religion, have rejected domination by the Church of England but without necessarily rejecting spirituality. Many have recognized spirituality as necessary to being human, just as salt is necessary for the body to survive. An understanding of spirituality as the source of energy or 'whatever floats your boat' may help prevent the depletion of the salt of natural spirituality in children thus ensuring that they flourish as human beings. Such understanding may also help an adult 'none' to explore their sense of God and faith. Furthermore the replacement of the external by an internal authority applies as much to Christians as to 'nones'. The Christian self turns to and acknowledges God who dwells within, thus grounding identity in that relationship, a process of which I speak from my own experience.

1 Abreu, L. & Sheard, S. (eds.) (2013) *Hospital Life: Theory and Practice from the Medieval to the Modern, (e-book), Proceedings from the 2011 conference of the International Network for the History of Hospitals*, Bern: Peter Lang AG.

2 Rawcliffe, C. (2013) 'Communities of the Living and of the Dead: Hospital Confraternities in the Later Middle Ages', in Bonfield, Reinarz and Huguet-Termes (eds) *Hospitals and Communities 1100–1960, Proceedings from the 2009 conference of the International Network for the History of Hospitals*, Bern: Peter Lang AG: 125–154.

3 Schneiders, S. (2005) 'Christian Spirituality: Definition, Methods and Types' in Sheldrake, P. (ed) *The New SCM Dictionary of Christian Spirituality*, London: SCM Press: 1–6.

4 Prayer which hopes for a deeper sense of God's presence, seeks union with God, often inspired by the Holy Spirit rather than using pre-set words.

5 Woods, R. and Tyler, P. (2012) 'Introduction: What is Christian Spirituality?' in Woods & Tyler (eds) *The Bloomsbury Guide to Christian Spirituality*, London: Bloomsbury Publishing: 1–6.

6 Schneiders, S. (2005) 'Christian Spirituality: Definition, Methods and Types' in Sheldrake, P. (ed) *The New SCM Dictionary of Christian Spirituality*, London: SCM Press:1–6.

7 Saint Augustine of Hippo, fourth century theologian and philosopher whose writings influenced the development of Western Christianity. Not to be confused with Saint Augustine of Canterbury, sixth century Benedictine monk and missionary to England, who became the first Archbishop of Canterbury in 597.

8 Hay, D. (2006) *Something There*, London: Darton, Longman & Todd: 31.

9 Hay, D. (2007) *Why Spirituality is Difficult for Westerners*, Exeter: Societas: 41.

10 Hay, D. and Nye, R. (2006) *The spirit of the child*, (revised ed.) London: Jessica Kingsley Publishers: 144–149.

11 Literally means the spirit of the times, a way of describing the character or prevailing culture of a particular time period.

12 Woodhead, L. (2016) 'Why "no religion" is the new religion.' The British Academy Lecture January 2016 http://www.britac.ac.uk/events/2016/Why_no_religion_is_the_new_religion.cfm

13 British Social Attitudes Survey 36 conducted in 2018 states 52%.

Food for thought

- *How do you understand spirituality?*
- *Which of piety, uniform prayer, the church, mystical prayer would Jesus describe as salt?*
- *Who or what are your main sources of spiritual nourishment? If you are not able to answer this question please do not fret – we shall come back to this later.*
- *What is your attitude to those who say they are 'spiritual but not religious'?*

Chapter three
Who do I think I am?

Introduction

Having described the changing role of Christianity since the Second World War and the more recent change in the influence of the Church of England in the formation of identity I now describe my personal experience. I hope that this personal illustration of the effect of external expectations on the development of my identity and my awareness of the changes of the 1960s will help your reflections. I then describe developments in the identity of the nursing profession to further illustrate the changes in how identity is formed.

The way we were…

Social historians tell us that at the start of the twentieth century church going or religious affiliation was the norm, but that only half of those born in the 1970s had any kind of church connection. If like me you grew up in the period between the Second World War and 1970 you will have lived through the change in the way we as individuals achieve identity. When I was growing up in the 1950s my family went to church – but we were unusual in a street of one hundred and fifty houses. My maternal grandparents had died before my mother married and had not been churchgoers. On the other hand my paternal grandparents were still alive and were and had always been churchgoers, or rather chapelgoers. That grandmother in particular had very rigid views on most things including church attendance. She refused to miss her chapel service in order to babysit for my parents so that they might go to a special service at their church. Her identity was forged through duty and doing what she saw as the right thing, which included attendance at chapel, rather than in relationships. Unlike salt my grandmother's identity did little to care for others or help them flourish.

Growing up in this milieu my identity was created by other people. It was like putting on clothes not of my own choosing but given me by well-meaning others. These others were parents, grandparents, other relatives, the church and its minister, school teachers, and society – or rather 'people', as feared in the expression 'What will people think?' My life and my identity were shaped according to external expectations, emanating from these supposed authorities. I have described how the power of these authorities waned during the 1960s so individuals were now free to develop an identity based on their own subjective experiences. Academics have referred to this as 'the turn to the subjective'. In the 1960s we learnt that our subjective experiences are both valid and valuable. Furthermore we learnt that the external expectations not only lacked authority but that even their supposed authority was without foundation. We had been led to believe that those expectations were of God. In the 1960s we discovered that they were not so much of God but of the institution, the Church, which had conveyed the expectations. What we had assumed was salt was a fake, or a substitute containing mostly potassium chloride.

Some readers will feel that their external expectations came from parents but how did they rationalize their domination? Did they, like my father, refer to 'honour your father and your mother'? If so, what lay behind this reference? A lively faith and active knowledge of the Bible or what they had been taught by the Church or learnt by rote in Sunday School? Was this genuine salt or a substitute?

The turn to the subjective was indeed the turn away from the hierarchical but this was not necessarily a turn away from God but a turn away from the dominant other that had taken God's place. For me, casting off that domination released the ability to take responsibility for myself and for my relationship with God. I could, if I so chose, acknowledge that God dwells within me, befriend my personal desires and become the person God made me to be. My dominant other whom I cast off was my father but I recognized that he was channelling his own mother whose ideas and thoughts were confined to her understanding of what she believed she had been taught. However, it would seem that for many people the dominant other was the religion of the institutional Church which had provided what sociologists refer to as a sacred canopy, 'a sheltering fabric of security and answers for both the profound and the mundane questions of human life'[1]. The sacred canopy of the Church answered all the questions and supplied all the reasons thereby removing any need to think for oneself. Under such a canopy certain people and professions were tacitly recognized as having significance, supposedly giving them justification for their dominance. We might have referred to those people as 'the great and the good' and they comprised the aristocracy, the Lords of the Manor and professions such as medical Consultants and Barristers.

By the 1970s the significant people were still likely to be members of the professions such as medicine and the law, but teachers and clergy might well be included. More significantly the Lords of the Manor were no longer necessarily aristocrats but were now those who lived in the biggest houses in a community. Of course some professional people lived in the biggest houses! However, at the same time, society was changing. Houses were bought by in-comers who were not bothered about being 'significant' – nor were they recognized as such. My husband and I are a good example of this phenomenon. We moved to our present house in the 1980s. The previous occupants had been regarded as 'significant people' but the community was undecided about us. Our house was 'significant' but we were both graduates who worked in industry – we did not fit the accepted profile!

Back in the 1950s the personal and professional identity of the significant people, (doctors, clergy, lawyers, Lords of the Manor) was formed according to external expectations. Their personal identity supported their professional identity which in turn bolstered their personal identity. If you have read or seen films of crime stories of that era you will have noticed the tacit understanding 'he could not have done it – he's a doctor,' or 'he's a pillar of the community – he's the chief constable.' Anybody who was not part of the establishment, not a 'significant' person, forged their personal and professional identity according to external expectations which were based on Christianity. However, as the influence of Christianity waned so the external expectations changed as may be seen in developments in the nursing profession since the founding in 1948 of the National Health Service (NHS).

Professional & personal identity: the modern nursing profession
Whilst the introduction of the NHS was 'one of the outstanding achievements of the UK's history in the 20th century' bringing change to the delivery of healthcare, some of the component parts of the service retained traditional roles: 'You still had Florence Nightingale values then and matron and sister had real authority'[2]. Not only was paternalism, albeit in feminine form, present but power was seen to be exercised: nurses 'had to obey matron in their private life as well, taking instructions on how late they could stay out, how smartly dressed they were and the suitability of any young man they wished to marry – although getting married meant leaving the job.' Nurses were trained in hospital-based schools which often included accommodation requiring specified behaviour patterns. There were indications that intimidation was the means of control and personal identity was constrained by the requirements of the profession.

The decade of the 1960s found 'nurses were starting to feel more confident within the brave new world of healthcare and beginning to develop greater independence'[3]. Matron was still a powerful figure at the beginning of the1960s but the Salmon Report of 1966 marked the beginning of the end of her traditional role. Hierarchy was still in evidence in the control of nurses' lives (the age of majority was 21 until 1970), in separation by rank in the dining room with doctors having their own dining room and in a general respect for the position rather than the person: 'You didn't walk through a door in front of somebody more senior than you.' Nurses described their lives in the 1960s as 'regimented' compared with today but everybody knew their role, even the Consultants – the deference paid by a consultant to Matron in the 1967 film Carry on Doctor was not entirely unrealistic.

In the 1970s the strict discipline that had ensured the smooth running of the wards was being relaxed and nurses were no longer like cogs in a machine. Patients were encouraged to use nurses' first names and ward sisters were asked to consider nursing staff's requests for time off when planning duty rotas. The constraints on the nurse's personal identity were starting to disappear. However, the old hierarchy had not disappeared: one nurse remembered her first day on the ward as part of her training, which she thought meant learning by asking questions. She was firmly told that she was not there to ask questions but should do as she was told.

One nurse observed that the 1970s was a changing environment where 'People were beginning to see nursing not as a vocation but almost as a stepping stone to something else,'[4]. The decline of the Christian influence meant the loss of the legal and social rules which defined nursing as a vocation, so professional identity was changing and in 1972 the Briggs Committee suggested that nursing required a degree. The shift away from vocation released nurses from vocational obligations and compliance with hierarchy to the extent that they were no longer afraid to challenge what they felt was wrong with the health service. There were strikes for better pay and the Royal College of Nursing (RCN) became a trade union in 1976.

The 1980s were characterised by staff protests giving further credence to the argument that individual identity was no longer determined by 'the complex web of legally and socially accepted rules which governed individual identity in Christian Britain'[5]. The year 1983 saw the establishment of a regulatory council to set standards and guidelines for nurse education[6] and in 1986 Project 2000 started the move to diploma level nurse training based in colleges and universities rather than in hospital based schools[7]. Thus education was replacing vocation for professional identity.

Practice nursing boomed in the 1990s and a lot of previously entirely medical sacred ground, such as running clinics, prescribing, ordering investigations, was claimed by nurses, thus challenging the status quo[8]. In the millennium years specialist nursing posts increased with nurses taking charge of functions, such as minor injuries, previously carried out by junior doctors[9]. There were even practices run by nurses who hired doctors!

In 2008 the Nursing and Midwifery Council ratified proposals to make nursing an all-graduate profession and in 2009 the health minister announced that all new nurses would have to have a degree from 2013. It seems that confidence in personal identity was fuelling confidence in professional identity and seriously challenging the established way of doing things. However, financial matters caused hospital managements to require evidence of efficacy and nurses once again found themselves complying with external expectations. They demonstrated a high level of skill and a defined body of knowledge which is passed on to trainees in establishments controlled by the profession. They produced evidence that their knowledge is not static but always increasing through research. Furthermore state registration is required and mandatory for employment, and nursing is self-regulating with its own code of ethics. Thus nurses escaped the external expectations and control of the traditional paternalistic system but took on external expectations of skill, knowledge and ethics defined by their own hierarchy.

Summary

The rejection of the hierarchical and paternalistic aspects of the Christian dominant culture, the recognition of the false salt, meant that those constraints for constructing identity were no longer present. The authority of the self meant defining my own identity. Gone was the traditional acceptance of 'this is how we do things'. Other examples of such challenges to the dominant culture's way of thinking and doing are Alistair Campbell's work on pastoral care which started in 1964[10], Elisabeth Kübler-Ross's work on death and dying[11], and Cicely Saunders' development of the hospice concept in the late 1950s and early 1960s[12] challenging not only the paternalism of the medical profession but also the dominant culture of the medical model. All three privileged the person over the system – the person was to be served by the system and the system should be modified when and where necessary in order to maintain the prime importance of the person. These are examples of salt caring for individuals and enabling them to flourish.

Of course the supreme example of the privileging of the person over the system is found in Jesus. In Matthew 12 we see that the disciples' hunger is more important than keeping the law. Likewise to heal the man with the withered hand is more important than keeping the law. Jesus illustrates the point with the example that they would lift their only sheep out of a pit on the Sabbath and how much more valuable is a human being than a sheep. This reference to value reminds us of today's financial constraints which make it hard for us to recognize when and where we are failing to privilege the person over the system. We set out with good intentions of being effective salt but fail to recognize when we have lost our flavour. To further illustrate and help us identify these situations we'll consider the changing role of the patient in the healthcare system.

1 Kurtz in Thomas, J. (1997) 'The most serious charge sociology can make against theologians is that they have failed to provide the cultural means of generating religious commitment' What concepts are most valuable in the service of Christian believing and belonging? (Unpublished assignment for MTh.)

2 O'Dowd, A. (2008a) 'NHS Nursing in the 1950s' Nursing Times 10 January 2008 http://www.nursingtimes.net/nhs-nursing-in-the-1950s/461928.article

3 O'Dowd, A. (2008b) 'Nursing in the 1960s : "The ward sisters were pretty fierce"' Nursing Times 4 February 2008 http://www.nursingtimes.net/nursing-in-the-1960s-the-ward-sisters-were-pretty-fierce/577485.article

4 O'Dowd. A. (2008c) 'Nursing in the 1970s: "You are here to do the work, so get on with it".' Nursing Times 3 March 2008 http://www.nursingtimes.net/nursing-in-the-1970s-you-are-here-to-do-the-work-so-get-on-with-it/849257.article

5 Brown, C. (2009) The Death of Christian Britain, (2nd ed.), London: Routledge: 8

6 O'Dowd. A. (2008d) 'Nursing in the 1980s' Nursing Times 8 April 2008 http://www.nursingtimes.net/nursing-in-the-1980s/108415.article

7 Thomas, B.Gail (2016) 'A brief History of Nursing in the UK' https://memoriesofnursing.uk/wp-content/uploads/A-Brief-History-of-Nursing-in-the-UK.pdf

8 O'Dowd. A. (2008e) 'Nursing in the 1990s' Nursing Times 12 May 2008 http://www.nursingtimes.net/whats-new-in-nursing/nursing-in-the-1990s/1330344.article

9 O'Dowd. A. (2008f) 'Millennium Nursing' Nursing Times 30 May 2008 http://www.nursingtimes.net/millennium-nursing/1437673.article

10 Campbell, A. (1986) Rediscovering Pastoral Care, (2nd ed.), London: DLT.

11 Kübler-Ross, E. (1969) On death and dying, London: Tavistock Publications.

12 du Boulay, S. (2007) Cicely Saunders The Founder of the Modern Hospice Movement, (expanded ed.) London: SPCK.

Food for thought

• What external expectations operate today?

• Describe other professions and/or institutions in which the external expectations continue to operate.

• Remind yourself of your earlier consideration of the external expectations that influenced the formation of your identity. Has your response changed? If so, how?

• What social pressures inhibit your identity development?

• Have the external expectations previously found in institutional Christianity and a paternalistic society been replaced by expectations derived from social media?

- *Identify Christian influences found in attitudes and decision-making today.*
- *Are you already identifying examples of the system being more important than the person? If so, where?*
- *Does your church privilege the system/organisation over the person or the person over the system?*

Chapter four

Our stories are who we are

Introduction

Examining our role as salt, preserving and bringing out God's flavour in creation, we have identified the influence of external expectations on identity development. Only when the power of those expectations declined and personal subjective experience was acknowledged as valuable were individuals able to develop their identity for themselves. They were able not only to tell their own story but that story was who they were. 'Separated from our stories, we lose our identity'[1]. Our stories are our identity, not merely descriptions of the self but they are the self, being perpetually recreated according to experience and circumstance. When someone says 'tell me about yourself' we talk about who we are and what we do – we tell our story. Many people think that they create the stories themselves, not realizing that stories are often offered by or inherited from family, friends, literature and the media. If you are a Terry Pratchett fan you may recall his description: 'Stories, great flapping ribbons of shaped space-time, have been blowing and uncoiling around the universe since the beginning of time'[2]. As we develop our identity we actively choose our story. Whether inherited, borrowed or home-grown it is our story, it is who we are. However if we lose that story we may become passive, the object in someone else's story. Equally as we live our own story we may consciously or unconsciously damage or even destroy somebody else's story, thus making them an object in our story. In so doing we challenge the other person's sense of who they are, their purpose and value, causing them to question their identity. To illustrate this I am going to describe what has happened over time to the identity of the healthcare patient which also reveals the changing nature of the salt of care.

Medieval healthcare – the patient versus the provider

It is not surprising that until very recently it was thought that mediaeval hospitals were founded and run by Christian religious orders[3]. It seems appropriate that these orders should have been the salt of the earth, preserving and bringing out God's flavour in creation by caring for others. The medieval patient might be suffering a disease, might be a leper, or might equally be a traveller. One way or another he would be sick and poor, for those who had money did not go to hospital but were treated at home[4]. The television series based on Ken Follett's book *World without End* presents a reasonable idea of what was happening before the Reformation took place. Christianity, or at least Christianity as taught by the Church, seeped into every aspect of life. The hospitals were not large like our hospitals today but small. Patients were regarded as temporary members of a spiritual community – at that time the word 'spiritual' meant 'religious' and religion in England was Christianity. A picture of the medieval hospital ward shows the crucifix at the end of the 'ward' or infirmary, for these hospitals were to be found in monasteries. No doubt the motive was a duty of care as found in Jesus's words:

> For I was hungry and you gave me something to eat, I was thirsty and you gave me something to drink, I was a stranger and you invited me in, I needed clothes and you clothed me, I was sick and you looked after me, I was in prison and you came to visit me. *Matthew 25:35–36*

Patients were expected to join in with the monastic offices (services) and they earned their keep, as it were, by praying for the imperiled souls of the rich. In this scenario the patient's identity is not individual but is part of the story of the monastery which acted like salt providing the care.

However, recent research has established that religious orders were not the only people to found hospitals. Whilst it is true that a lot of the evidence was lost or destroyed due to the actions of Henry VIII and the Reformation nevertheless it is now known that in medieval times small hospitals were also founded by an individual or a group of individuals. Bishops, lords, archdeacons, townsmen all founded hospitals to look after the sick-poor, the diseased, travellers, lepers. They also distributed food to the needy – bread and beer referred to as 'dole'. For example in 1249 Bishop Suffield personally founded the hospital of St Giles, Norwich, not on behalf of the Church, not only out of sympathy for the poor and sick, but also 'to secure the remission of his sins'[5]. However, the great majority of alms-givers to this particular hospital were 'ordinary laymen and women from towns and villages scattered across Norfolk,' some of whom lacked a surname[6]. The idea of purgatory and hell may seem strange to us today but their influence in medieval times is not to be underestimated for it caused individuals and small groups to found and support hospitals, not to save lives but rather 'to exercise charity'. We might say that they were trying to show that they were the salt of the earth referred to by Jesus.

Apparently the care of the patient or inmate was almost incidental to the opportunity for the demonstration of piety, or proving one's saltiness. In founding the hospital the pious medieval man was focused on his own religious or spiritual status, not that of the patient. The pious man was concerned with his identity, his story – that of the patient was only relevant as someone who needed alms. Without the opportunity to give alms the pious man would have had to construct a different personal identity, a different story to illustrate his piety or saltiness. Once again the patient has no individual identity but is crucial to the identity of the pious man, whose saltiness may be questionable.

Reformation and beyond – the unsightly patient

With the advent of the Reformation and the Dissolution of the Monasteries many hospitals disappeared, resulting in many sick, disabled and helpless people being without shelter. In London the presence of so many destitute people on the streets caused the Lord Mayor to petition King Henry to let the civil authority have the old hospital buildings. At first sight this appears to be another expression of the Christian duty of care expressed in Matthew 25. However the motivation was as much removal of the destitute from public places, and therefore out of sight, as it was to improve their situation. Such motivation casts doubt on the saltiness of the care.

No longer a part of a spiritual monastic community, these institutions were still run by a clergyman (hospitaller or chaplain). Services were replaced by religious instruction, for the chaplain was charged with responsibility for the salvation of the 'lewd and naughty' patients[7]. The identity projected onto the patient was of someone who did not know how to behave so needed disciplining to become compliant to authority. The patient was unsightly so needed to be kept from the gaze of the better-off. This patient was seen as an object which needed to be out of sight but would benefit from the care offered. In light of the motive to what extent is the care offered an expression of salt? Might this be an example of salt losing its flavour? Lest we think that this is an historical problem there are contemporary parallels such as the council in Windsor debating the plight of the homeless, not just as a response to their need but also in view of the royal nuptials which took place in the town in 2018.

Nineteenth century financial constraints changed the character of hospitals so that they only admitted patients who were respectable and could be easily cured. People suffering from venereal disease, such as prostitutes, and those who needed long-term care were not admitted. Neither were the dying as they could not be cured and the length of stay was unpredictable. In short care was only offered to a respectable being who would be cured or mended in a short period of time, but this patient was still the object of the medical profession's attention, with a role in the story of the hospital. Those who did not fulfil the criteria for hospital care were excluded from the healthcare story. Is the presence of the salt of the earth limited? Does the salt of care discriminate?

Twentieth century – the patient versus the system
The twentieth century saw change in 1948 with the introduction of the National Health Service (NHS) in which everyone was entitled to healthcare. The 1970s saw the introduction of 'individualized care', entailing patient choice and autonomy, which gained ground in the 1980s and was finally established in the Patients' Charter of 1991[8]. At last it appears that the patient is no longer an object that needs something doing to it but a subject who chooses his care. However, the population profile has aged and the financial strain on the NHS is a considerable concern. Despite financial constraints hospitals today still cure and mend whilst dying is not their strong suit. Curing and mending has led once again to a tendency to objectivise the patient, that is to treat them as an object, referring to 'the broken leg in bed six' or 'the pneumonia in bed two' rather than naming the person.

This medical model of care or 'cure and mend' gives the patient a diagnostic identity which makes her the subordinate half of a power relationship. Her story changes without her realizing it – the very institution of the hospital puts her on the receiving end of authority (or power) of doctors, physiotherapists, nurses, for which she feels she must be grateful. Until recently the taking of a medical history was considered to be the story – my Medical Consultant daughter says this is still the case and the process frequently curtails, subverts or even prevents the patient's story. The method of taking a medical history ensures that what might be termed the 'uncomfortable' parts of the story are omitted – that is uncomfortable for the nurse or doctor taking the history. The omitted uncomfortable parts may be personal tragedies, events seemingly unrelated to the illness which the patient deems significant, or lengthy asides when the doctor has other patients to visit. However, these parts are important, even vital to the patient. The omission damages the patient's story and reduces her from the subject of the medical history to the object of the enquiry. She needs those parts to be spoken and heard as part of the development of a new, revised story which takes into account, but is not dominated by, the illness. Does this kind of care enable the patient to flourish?

Revising the story

There are many reasons, apart from illness, why the identity story may need to be revised. Bereavement, financial disaster, divorce, long-term treatment, burglary can all disrupt the person's story and affect their sense of identity. Not only does the story need revising to accommodate the event it also needs to repair any damage caused by the event. To restore the person's sense of who they are they need to feel in control of their story – that they are telling it rather than being on the receiving end. Meaning and significance need to be restored and seen to be active even when the disruption of the identity story is the diagnosis of a terminal illness[9].

Sometimes people need help to see themselves outside the confines of the crisis – whether it be illness, job loss, divorce, a death. Rather than amend their story they may need to create a new story, to develop a new identity. Being secure in the new story, and therefore secure in their new identity helps them to avoid being on the receiving end of a story not of their own making. Those who are vulnerable to this kind of imposition are those who are ill or incapacitated in any way. Their vulnerability arises from the fact that various professionals will come to 'do something' to them, to ease their pain or manage their symptoms or provide care. Their relationship with these professionals is not equal, they are the object of professional attention, and therefore physically, emotionally, spiritually disadvantaged. They need to be able to identify and resist these external expectations.

Equally problematic may be the well-meaning 'friends' who come with advice – for the person they knew, that is in their earlier identity. These friends will not be aware of the new identity that has been developed so the person needs to be secure enough in the new identity not to slip back into being what the other person expects them to be. We too need to be sensitive with those we meet, not to impose on them what we think they should be or do. Rather it is we who by God's grace may be or do what they need at that time. Just as Jesus met people where they were, making no judgement on where he thought they should be, so we too are to accept people as they are, where they are and without telling them what we think they should be or do. Like the salt we are not the focus but in our being we care for and bring out the flavour of others.

Summary
In the medieval period care was an act of Christian duty and a way of demonstrating piety. From the Reformation to the nineteenth century the provision of care was influenced by a need for social control. Then financial constraints restricted care to those who could be cured or mended. The twentieth century saw the reversal of this policy with the introduction of care for all in the NHS. The patient is in turn a player in the story of the monastery, the means by which a pious man may save his soul, an unsightly object to be removed from the streets, or a depersonalized being to be cured or mended. By the twentieth century 'the medical model' of cure and mend, tended to see patients as problems needing solutions, rather than as people who need and deserve love and care. Therefore the patient has to deal with both the onslaught and deprivations of physical illness and the loss of the

sense of self with its threat to personal identity. Such a patient is in need of care/salt to restore life.

We have seen the role that story plays in identity but a story, any story, requires a listener. If we are wanting people to come to know Jesus as we ourselves know Jesus then we are going to have to listen. The question is 'What are we listening for?' To recognize where God is in someone else's life I need to know and be able to talk about where God is in my life.

1 Guenther, M. (1992) *Holy Listening* London: Darton, Longman & Todd: 149.

2 Pratchett, T. (1992) *Witches Abroad* London: Corgi: 12.

3 Cobb, M. (2005) *The Hospital Chaplain's Handbook*: a guide for good practice Norwich: Canterbury Press: 1–3.

4 Rawcliffe, C. (2013) 'Communities of the Living and of the Dead: Hospital Confraternities in the Later Middle Ages', in Bonfield, Reinarz and Huguet-Termes (eds) *Hospitals and Communities 1100–1960, Proceedings from the 2009 conference of the International Network for the History of Hospitals* Bern: Peter Lang AG: 125–154.

5 Bonfield, C.(2013) 'An Online Community: A Case Study of the 3DReconstruction and Web-based Guide to the Great Hospital, Norwich', in Bonfield, Reinarz & Huguet-Termes (eds) *Hospitals and Communities 1100–1960, Proceedings from the 2009 conference of the International Network for the History of Hospitals* Bern: Peter Lang AG: 389–411.

6 Rawcliffe, C. (2013) 'Communities of the Living and of the Dead: Hospital Confraternities in the Later Middle Ages', in Bonfield, Reinarz and Huguet-Termes (eds) *Hospitals and Communities 1100–1960, Proceedings from the 2009 conference of the International Network for the History of Hospitals* Bern: Peter Lang AG: 125–154.

7 Swift, C. (2014) *Hospital Chaplaincy in the Twenty-first Century, 2nd Edition*, Farnham: Ashgate: 21–27.

8 Woodward, V. (1998) 'Caring, patient autonomy and the stigma of paternalism', *Journal of Advanced Nursing* 28 (5): 1046–1052.

9 Williams, J. (2007) Sixth Norman Autton Memorial Lecture
http://audio.cofemedia.org.uk/synod/JaneWilliams6November.mp3
Text: http://www.nhs-chaplaincy-spiritualcare.org.uk/normanautton6lecture.htm

Food for thought

- *In medieval times the need for spiritual or religious healing was recognized and even given precedence over physical healing. To what*

extent do we today recognize the need for spiritual healing?
- *To what extent can you identify with the medieval man concerned to prove his piety?*
- *How and/or where is the Christian duty of care found today?*
- *Does the Church/do Christians hide behind the Welfare State in the expression of care?*
- *What motivates people today to care?*
- *Does care/salt/the Holy Spirit discriminate?*
- *Does the church give its members an equivalent to the diagnostic identity, seeing them as problems needing solutions rather than as people who need and deserve love and care?*
- *Does the church see people as the solution to a problem like clearing the gutters, cleaning the church, providing money?*

Chapter five
Where is God in your life?

'How dare we invite someone to explore their spirituality if we have not explored our own?'[1]

Introduction

Earlier I recommended thinking of spirituality not in the somewhat academic terms of the means by which we find 'transcendent meaning and aspiration' but as 'whatever floats your boat', 'what makes you tick.' Spirituality is where and how we find meaning and purpose, it is the drive that makes us human which we are born with. In that earlier section I also asked how you understood spirituality and who or what were your main sources of spiritual nourishment, saying not to worry if you could not answer the question because we would return to it. For all of us there are times when we struggle to acknowledge that God can work and speak, through anyone and anything. What is more He can feed us in whatever way is appropriate for each of us at any given time in our lives. He can nourish us through other people, through experiences, through music, art, nature, sport. Our difficulty is that we don't recognize how we are fed so we cannot say where God is in our lives. If we cannot recognize God in our own lives how are we to be the salt that helps others recognize God in their lives? Here I offer some exercises and reflections that may help us understand our own spirituality and recognize how God nourishes us.

Recognizing God in your life

As we are each unique beings the balance and nature of forms of nourishment will be different for each of us. The different approaches to daily devotion illustrate this point admirably. Some will follow the lectionary and others will use bible-reading notes. Some will use a formal service like Morning Prayer from Celebrating Common Prayer. Others will use extempore prayer, some will use set prayers or a prayer guide and still others will sit in silence. One hospice chaplain likened his silent prayer to two lovers sitting by a river together – they do not need to speak because they are just happy to be in each other's presence. During the course of his day he took time out in the hospice chapel, where he was both lover and the beloved and was nourished without the use of words. Without this experience, which we might term contemplation, he had no fuel for his actions. In effect contemplation sustained his actions giving him energy and strength to be alongside and support the patients. Recognizing when we do not have what it takes to be alongside someone takes courage but if we don't take a step back we may harm ourselves and/or those whom we seek to help.

One way of recognizing God in your life is to do a **lifeline exercise**:

Take a large piece of paper, preferably A3, and draw a line diagonally across it. At bottom left write 'birth' and then if you are under forty mark the years in fives at 5cm/2inch intervals up to your present age. If you are over forty mark the years in tens at 10cm/4inch intervals up to your present age. Mark major experiences and events on the timeline. Write a few words to denote each experience above the timeline for things which were basically creative or positive, below the timeline for experiences which were initially difficult or negative. Where a difficult or negative experience became creative use a vertical arrow across the timeline to indicate the transformation. Then ask the Holy Spirit to show you where God was present in the experiences. Then ask the Holy Spirit to bring to your mind other experiences where God was present. It is helpful to let this exercise run for several days so that experiences can surface.

You may find it helpful to consider the things you like to do, your hobbies and sporting activities, and ask yourself whether God is with you in these activities. Ask yourself what these activities do for you – is it possible that God is not only with you but is nourishing you in these activities? The **dinner-plate** exercise may help your reflection:

Think of your favourite meal. What are the equivalents to the parts of this meal in terms of activities that energize you (even if they exhaust you as well). I have known people name their favourite activity but when I ask how often they do it they admit that they have not done it for months. One friend told me he loved kayaking but then admitted that he had not been on the water for six months. Then he realized that he had not been to a concert for some time either and observed that his self-care was pretty poor and wasn't it good that God was merciful! In marked contrast a lady of my acquaintance who is both vicar and hospice chaplain is happy to tell everyone about being nourished by God, not just in prayer and scripture which we might expect but also when she goes horse-riding – and she makes sure she goes every Saturday! Her appearance tells others that she is living life to the full – flourishing in the power of the Holy Spirit who, by her own admission, is why she fulfils and enjoys doing both jobs.

Another way of becoming aware of God in everyday life is using what Ignatius of Loyola called the **Examen of Consciousness** – this means examining our awareness or consciousness of God's presence[2]. At the end of the day give yourself time to reflect. Begin by asking the Holy Spirit to show you what he wants you to see. Then look over the events of the day and ask God to show you where He was particularly present and give thanks. Consider what God may have been showing you or asking of you this day. Consider your feelings: joy/pain, harmony/disquiet, freedom/restriction, love/anger, presence of God/absence of God. What is God asking you to focus on? Can you identify any negative attitude that prevented you from responding to God's love? Ask the Holy Spirit to help you hand the negative to God, ask for forgiveness and receive His healing. Give thanks for the times where you have responded to God's love.

Draw your reflection to a close with a prayer for help and guidance for tomorrow.

Recognizing God in creation

There is a story of an elderly gentleman who stopped coming to church. When the vicar visited to see how he was he said that he could no longer find God in church but found Him out on the dales. Even when we do not share that experience we accept that God is in His creation, as Dorothy Gurney's poem says:

> The kiss of the sun for pardon,
> The song of the birds for mirth,
> One is nearer God's Heart in a garden
> Than anywhere else on Earth[2].

To help our awareness of God in creation we could make a **Walk of Awareness**, which like the Examen was devised by Ignatius. This can be undertaken in any space, from the smallest garden to the largest forest. Give yourself half an hour away from other people and begin as you would any time of prayer:

Be still and silent and take in the whole scene before you – breathe it in with your eyes, ears, nose, feet. Be aware of yourself, your limbs and your senses, as you walk. Be prepared to collect anything that seems significant to you – without needing to know why.

Use your eyes to notice all that is around you, in front and behind, to the sides, above and below. Notice colour, texture, shape, light and shade. Think what your sight means to you. What would your life be like without it? Give thanks in whatever way seems appropriate – a smile, spoken word, song, dance.

Use your ears to listen carefully, distinguishing the various sounds close by, far away and in the middle distance. Notice whether sounds are at your level, below or above and the feelings they elicit in you. Reflect on what your hearing means to you. What would your life be like without it? Give thanks in whatever way seems appropriate.

Use your nose to notice the smells – pleasant and unpleasant. Identify the sources of the smells if possible. Think what your sense of smell means to you. What would your life be like without it? Give thanks in whatever way seems appropriate.

Use your hands to touch some of the things you see. Feel the texture. Feel the ground through your feet, feel the air on your skin, the sun or rain on your face. Reflect on how we use touch: to show affection, to write, to play a musical instrument, to play a sport, to cook and clean… What would your life be like without the ability to touch? Give thanks in whatever way seems appropriate.

Taste some of the things you have seen – a blade of grass or a leaf, a blackberry or an apple. Reflect on the importance of taste. What would your life be like without a sense of taste? Give thanks in whatever way seems appropriate.

Before you end your walk try to form one mental picture that will remind you of this experience. Give thanks to God whose love endures forever.

Recognizing God in buildings and constructions
When we say that we believe that God is present in all of His creation we tend to focus on the natural world as in the Walk of Awareness. However, we must be careful not to ignore or dismiss God in constructed items like buildings, ships, planes, cars and as for seeing Him in other people – well that's another matter!

Recognizing God in other people
At time of writing some research has shown that hip surgery patients

given attention by someone sitting with them make a much quicker recovery than those left to their own devices. The consequent saving to the NHS was noteworthy – all for the sake of human contact in the form of social interaction. When we have little contact with other people we soon lose our sense of purpose, which leads to loss of interest which leads to feelings of worthlessness. What value is there in going on living?

There is a story of an elderly Scottish gentleman who stopped going to church. When the minister visited he was sitting by the open fire. One of the hot glowing coals fell out of the fire. As it sat on the hearth it cooled losing its glow. The minister took the fire-tongs, picked up the coal and placed it back in the fire where it warmed up and started to glow again. The following week the gentleman was in church. We are like that coal because without meeting and friendship with other Christians we lose our glow. This is not saying that other Christians make our identity – that would be back to external expectations. Rather God nourishes us through other people especially when they share their experiences of God in their lives. To help you identify how God nourishes you through people try the **Radiators & Drains** exercise:

Make a list of friends and family. It does not need to be exhaustive. Then look through the list and think about how you feel when you are with or talk to each person. Mark them as an 'R' for radiator if they make you feel valued or a 'D' for drain if they exhaust you or make you feel flat. Some people will be both – try to identify the situations in which they are radiators and those in which they are drains.

I used this exercise with several different groups of staff in the hospice. The bereavement counselors were very forthcoming about who in their lives was a radiator and who a drain and how they behaved in relation to each. One counsellor caused great hilarity when she said that she did not have any problems with drains as she had got rid of anybody who might be a drain! Needless to say I am not recommending this response!

Exploring our spirituality through scripture

There is no right or wrong way to learn about our spiritual selves through scripture – different approaches suit different people. Here I have summarised two approaches:

Lectio divina or divine reading is the practice of reading a passage of scripture and being prepared for a word or a phrase to touch us deeply or even jump out at us. We then ask God to guide us as we hold that word/phrase in our mind and heart and meditate on it. Some people refer to this practice as rumination – as cows chew the cud so we chew on the word of God in order to learn more about God in our lives. We then let the word/phrase lead our response – we pray. Finally we reflect, guided by the Holy Spirit we contemplate the significance of the experience. We may find it helpful to talk it through with a soul-friend or spiritual director.

Alternatively we may meditate on a passage of scripture or a story. First of all we read it through and then ask God to help us to enter the scene, to be there, perhaps to be one of the characters or perhaps a fly on the wall. As you read the passage again notice your reactions, your feelings. It is helpful if the passage is read by another person as I can then concentrate on my reactions and responses. For a guided meditation the passage is read aloud by another person who, on the second reading, intersperses the text with questions inspired by the Holy Spirit. In the Appendix I have given a couple of examples of guided meditation. If you use them on your own try to make a note of what you learnt, your reactions, feelings, thoughts, and talk them through with a soul-friend or spiritual director.

Summary

Issues which express what it is to be human and contribute to our sense of well-being, such as meaning, hope, purpose, connectedness and love were once expressed in religious language. In our increasingly secular society such language is disappearing from everyday vocabulary and we lack words to express the essence of our humanity, our spirituality[4].

I have offered a variety of exercises to help recognize our spirituality and how we are spiritually nourished. None of these exercises is better than others – what helps one person does not help another and vice versa. Neither is this a comprehensive range, for all these exercises may be undertaken on your own. There are many more group exercises, some of which involve creative activities. The important point is that in finding and understanding how God nourishes us, what gives our life meaning, we equip ourselves to be salt, helping others recognize what sustains them. In this way we help preserve and bring out the flavour of life even in those who do not acknowledge their spiritual needs, even in those who say they have no faith. We are effectively being the salt that they need.

1 Question asked by hospice chaplains whom I interviewed for my doctoral research.
2 Sheldrake, P. (ed.) (1991) *The Way of Ignatius Loyola* London: SPCK.
3 Gurney, D.F. (1913) 'God's garden' in *Poems*, London: Country Life.
4 Swinton, J. and Pattison, S., (2010) 'Moving beyond clarity: towards a thin, vague, and useful understanding of spirituality in nursing care', *Nursing Philosophy*, Vol 11: 226–237.

Food for thought
• *Did you undertake the exercises? Which did you find helpful? Which were unhelpful?*
• *If you did not undertake any of the exercises, why not?*
• *What social pressures inhibit your recognition and expression of your spirituality?*
• *What have you learnt about how God nourishes you?*
• *What have you learnt about your own spirituality?*

Chapter six

Don't just do something: sit there

Introduction

When we consider the circumstances of Jesus's birth we see that many people wanted or expected a Messiah/Saviour who would remove the Roman occupation. They wanted and expected the Messiah to be a military-style leader and it is clear that Jesus did not conform to their expectations. The point is that in sending Jesus God was providing the person humanity needed, not the person the people wanted or thought they needed. One of my hospice friends told me the story of the Jewish patient for whom the hospice chef, who was also Jewish, obtained kosher food. However, the patient wanted pork sausages! The son, who'd come from some distance to visit, was very devout and wanted to do the right thing for his father, so he rang his rabbi to ask what Psalms he should read and what prayers he should say. His father did not want any of that, he just wanted his son to be there. In fact he needed his son to be there – to say goodbye. Am I /are we being what is needed? Or am I/ are we being what we think and believe is needed – in other words are we following our own agenda? Or am I/ are we trying to be what other people tell us they want? Here I consider the attitudes of Christians, individually and in churches, to those not yet acknowledging Jesus Christ as Lord and Saviour.

Do Christians objectify non-Christians?

Previously I described the changing identity of the patient and referred to the way the medical profession gives patients a diagnostic identity, regarding them as objects to be mended or cured rather than as people in need of love and care. It is easy to criticise the medical profession but are we – individual Christians and Churches – sure we do not objectify others? Many years ago I met a lady who was in great distress because her closest friend, who did not know Jesus, was dying in a hospice. She had told her friend that she needed to be saved before she died and the friend had not been in the least bit interested. This meant that the lady's own need, to see her friend saved, was not fulfilled. She was not able to accept that just sitting with her friend, being a loving presence in an hour of need, was what was needed. We may long for family and friends to know Jesus as we do, but our enthusiasm may blind us to them as people and it may also have a negative effect. The timing is best left to God and actions may speak louder than words.

A hospice chaplain friend of mine told of a conversation with an evangelical ordinand on placement in the hospice. The conversation went like this:

Ordinand: do you tell them about the love of Christ?

Chaplain: Sometimes but not generally in our first meeting.

Ordinand: but you must tell them that they need to be saved…

Chaplain: No, that's your agenda. We work on their agenda.

I am not denying that the solution to the patient's problem is Jesus but I am saying that the ordinand's zeal for mission blinded him to the person. When the patient is someone we love or care about it is especially hard not to focus on saving their soul. Such a focus usually says more about the speaker than the patient.

Jesus's attitude to others: subject or object?

When we consider Jesus's actions in curing or mending people we see that they were not the object of his healing power. Not one of the people he healed became an object in his story but rather each was released as the subject of their own story, no longer bound by illness or sin. The woman who washed Jesus's feet, the woman taken in adultery, the woman at the well are all subjects in their own story. Each event glorifies God but not at the expense of the person – none of them becomes an object used to glorify. Rather each is a subject through whom God is glorified. Even the teachers of the law and Pharisees, described as white-washed tombs and as a brood of vipers, (Matthew 23:27&33) are subjects rather than objects. They are responsible for their own stories, their own actions, and will be judged accordingly.

Nowhere is there any suggestion that Jesus objectified people by seeing them as an opportunity to glorify God. Rather we are told that Jesus had compassion for people (Mark 6:34), he felt with them rather than like them. Compassion is not pity, nor is it sympathy, nor is it fixing – these would all objectify the person. Compassion is love which values people, treats each as the subject, and serves them in whatever way God directs.

Laying me and my story to one side and accepting the other where they are

In order to put us, human beings, first Jesus laid his divinity on one side. In order to put the person in front of me first I lay me, my self, on one side. In order to put the other person first I need to put my own concerns to one side – but if I don't know what those concerns are they may creep up on me and make it difficult for me to be present to others. At this point you may find it helpful to reflect on the exercises you undertook to recognize your spirituality.

A good test of whether I have successfully laid me to one side is my reaction, or rather my ability to not react, to beliefs, language, behaviour which are not part of my value system or not considered acceptable. To this list I might add appearance, disability, personal hygiene, halitosis and other characteristics which can challenge the Christian ability to love and value the other person. In the gospels we find numerous examples of Jesus reaching out with love, not reacting negatively, to people whose circumstances and or behaviour did not glorify God: the woman at the well (John 4:4–42), the woman taken in adultery (John 8:3–11), the man in the Gerasene cemetery (Luke 8:26–39), the boy with demons (Matthew 17:14–18) to name but a few.

Today, in order to accept and be alongside the person as and where they are, many hospice chaplains lay their distaste for smoking on one side – yes, hospices still have smoking rooms! Foul language is another issue which has to be ignored when listening to a patient's story. Then there are the risqué jokes – one of my friends never showed disapproval of the cigarettes or the risqué jokes so that gradually a trusting relationship was built, such that as he approached his death in hospital the old man asked for the hospice chaplain to be with him. When building a relationship eye contact is essential – and difficult if the person's appearance is unusual, ugly or dirty. Facial deformity, whatever the cause, is particularly difficult but eye contact is absolutely essential to affirm the person as a human being.

Accepting the other: without colluding or colliding

Arriving at the Day Unit I was met by a couple of the nursing staff who were both agitated about one particular patient. Then a complementary therapist appeared with the same concern. They knew the patient to be a church-goer but that day he had told them that he also believed, or rather knew, that there were fairies at the bottom of his garden. They were all convinced that it was my responsibility, as chaplain, to disabuse him of this idea. I asked them 'why?' Their answer: 'It's wrong, it's not right'. I asked: 'What harm is this belief doing him?' None that they could think of, but I went to speak with him to satisfy myself that he was still the same man I had spoken with the previous week. He told me that he realized he had upset the nurses with his talk of fairies but did not understand why. I neither supported his views on fairies nor contradicted them. After the patients had gone home I spoke with the concerned members of staff trying to enable them to identify why they were so distressed. I asked them to consider how they, healthy people without a terminal diagnosis, felt when someone tried to change their beliefs. Then they were able to consider what might happen if we had tried to change the beliefs of this terminally-ill patient. I explained that my role was not to change a person's spirituality or their spiritual beliefs but to support their spirituality without colluding or colliding. This is not to deny that I long for the person to know God's love as I do, but at this point my task is to demonstrate God's love by accepting and loving them as they are. My faith fuels and enables me to demonstrate acceptance and love but it is not stated in words. There is a sense in which I lay what I believe on one side in order to be God's love.

Summary

Just as salt is necessary for the preservation and flavour of food so the salt of the earth are necessary for the preservation and fullness of life of people. Facing any kind of difficulty, including approaching the end of life, people may think they want a cure, a remedy, a solution to their problem and they are surprised when they are given a listener and they are even more surprised that telling their story and being heard is actually helpful. They would never have said it was what they wanted but after the experience of being listened to they can acknowledge that it was what they needed. Speaker and listener have a common heritage in their humanity and it is this that is affirmed for both. Neither role is easy. It may have been years since the speaker told their story – even after a short space of time we may lose the ability and/or the will to tell our story. To listen is to lay one's own story on one side and be what the other person needs.

Food for thought

- Do you see non-Christians as people who need to be saved? If so, consider whether your attitude is compatible with their need to be loved.
- What is the church's view of non-Christians – are they people to be converted or people to be loved?
- Identify the problems you have accepting people as they are – different beliefs, language, behaviour, appearance, disability, personal hygiene. What might you do to help change your attitude?
- What is Jesus's attitude to people? Reflect on how each person is a subject through whom God is glorified but not at the expense of the person.

Chapter seven
Listening in colour

Introduction

Sound consultant Julian Treasure[1] argues that we are losing the ability to listen partly because our world is so noisy and partly because technical advances in recording equipment mean that accurate, careful listening is no longer appreciated. When running marriage preparation classes my husband and I set listening exercises for the couples. A favourite was for the man to take two minutes to explain the off-side rule in football to the lady. She would then tell him what she had heard. Her turn was to take two minutes on a shopping expedition which he then repeated – or not. Much hilarity was also caused by role-play demonstrations in which the body-language did not match the spoken word, but the point was made that listening takes effort and both partners need to feel that they are being listened to, they are heard.

From her experience in healthcare chaplaincy and in Spiritual Direction Margaret Guenther observes that 'not to be heard is not to be'[2] and she says that this is often the plight of the very young, the very old, the very sick, the confused and the dying. She notes that people no longer have the time or patience to listen, some are frightened of what they might hear and some dismiss the other as not worth listening to. A friend of mine, also a hospice chaplain, remarked that for many of the people he met being listened to was a very rare experience. Therefore he needed to be a 'holy listener' who did not classify or dismiss another person, but listened for the presence of God in the patient's story even when the patient was an atheist. It was then possible to encourage the patient to listen more deeply, to pay more attention to their own inner activity as they told their story. By the power of the Holy Spirit the listener may identify the speaker's spiritual strengths and weaknesses and be enabled to help him recognize those strengths and weaknesses.

The nature of listening

We have seen that becoming aware of my own spirituality is necessary for helping others to discover their spirituality. From my own experience I learn what to listen for. Those who have trained as Christian counsellors will be aware that the listener:

> will need to have made friends with the colourful spectrum
> of his own emotions if he is to become open and available to
> those of others[3].

At a conference of the British Association for the Study of Spirituality I met a Human Resources professional who was researching a doctorate which included the topic of listening. Her presentation referred to listening with the whole being, perceiving with the inner eye, listening with the inner ear and feeling with the spiritual heart[4]. She called it listening 'in full colour', rather than in black and white. Here is her account of her first experience of this type of listening which she describes as 'at a deeper level,' listening not just to the words but to the person.

> I was at a conference which began with an 'ice-breaker' or 'warm-up' exercise.
>
> The facilitator asked us to work, in pairs, with someone we had never met. We were invited to talk about our family, and then the other participant would tell us what they had heard.
>
> I was confident that I could listen well. I had worked in people

management jobs for some years and had interviewed hundreds. I started: "I have two brothers and a sister. My parents are still alive. They all live in Scotland. We will soon be having a party for my father's 70th birthday. He plays golf … etc etc. …"

I then expected my partner to start by saying, "You have two brothers….," perhaps getting some of the details wrong. (Pause) In fact, she began quite differently: "I am hearing that your family is very important to you. You might be a bit concerned about your father getting older, but he sounds fit – you mentioned golf."

This sent chills up my spine and the hair stood up on the back of my neck. How could she possibly know so much about me? I had never met her before, and she had no access to any information about my background.

At the time, it had not occurred to me that my family were important to me – in fact I had never thought about it. I had never considered what I 'felt' about them.

This was a different kind of listening than any I had encountered before. It was my first conscious experience of listening at a deeper level. Because my fellow participant had listened – not just to the words – but to the person, I was able to hear something *which I had always known* – (my family IS important to me) – but it was as if I was hearing it *for the very first time.*

Initially she was thrilled by the experience but later she expressed a note of caution: this type of listening needs handling with care lest it cause distress if the listener hears more than the person intended to convey, hears feelings which he was trying to conceal, or hears something completely different. I also have a concern about the bluntness of the listener's response: 'I am hearing that your family is very important to you.' A gentler approach might have been to ask the question 'am I hearing that your family is very important to you?' To make a statement about what I have heard risks belittling the value of both speaker and their experience.

In comparison with what we might call everyday listening this type of listening requires effort, skill and time and is easily dismissed as non-productive. Is it any surprise then that being listened to was a novel but welcome experience for many hospice patients? Is it just that we are too busy to listen to others or is there something about society's attitude to listening? Is our society supportive or dismissive of listening?

Society's attitude to listening

The novelty of the listening experience draws attention to the way in which listening is being devalued. Good listening is often associated with passivity, a lack of self-assertiveness and even a lack of self-esteem – when we cannot find anything good to say of someone we say 'He is a good listener'[5]. An acquaintance who worked as chaplain in a supermarket observed that five minutes being listened to might make all the difference for a member of staff. She also noted that absenteeism had declined since she had started working in the supermarket.

Listening is a natural process: we listen before we are born. When pregnant with my first child I noticed that the baby's movements changed whenever I played in an orchestra. On the several occasions when Saint-Saëns's Organ Symphony was performed the baby was most active. In today's society the emphasis is on successful communication and we assume that the meaning we receive is the message the speaker intends to convey. This approach views successful listening as the exchange of information, for example in the hospice the patient needs to convey successfully that the pain is worse in order to receive pain-killers. However, the hospice nurse should not assume that the pain is physical, and neither should she listen for her own self-interest so that the patient stops pressing the buzzer. Hospice chaplains described their role as 'really listening,' just 'being there with' the patient, listening and supporting. The difficulty in our result-oriented society is that this kind of listening does not produce results. It is not about the successful transmission of information and therefore has 'no remunerative value in our dominant culture'[6]. Given the importance of the role of story for identity do we, as society, realize that if listening has no value and therefore does not happen we as people have no value and struggle to exist.

Listening and identity

Has society come to the point where it sees no point in learning to listen because there is nothing to hear? If that is so, any sense of identity is denied and the individual is forced to find or justify identity in external factors and rules spoken by others. Identity is then controlled by those who speak the rules and there is no mutuality, for 'speaking is a way of asserting control and avoiding receptivity'[7]. We then have a subject-object situation, as described earlier, in which the individual is incapable of sustaining his own story. He cannot be the subject of his own story but must always be the object or a passing reference in someone else's story. In contrast, by listening I enable the speaker to find and tell his story. My listening shows that there is something to hear, and I am being what the person needs me to be. Thus the listener allows the other person to live, not as an object whose existence is dependent on others but as a subject in freedom. To listen is to value the story-teller or speaker. My daughter told me how when asking her ten-year-old daughter, my granddaughter, to do something she had to ask whether she had heard her. My granddaughter replied 'yes I heard you but I'm not listening.'

When Cicely Saunders founded the first of the modern hospices in 1967 her vision was to value people, including the dying, and her mantra 'You matter because you are you' spread around the world. In 1980 she was said to have brought humanity back into medicine[8] and yet in 2014 in the Reith lecture Atul Gawande, Harvard professor of medicine, surgeon, writer, thinker and political analyst, made a plea for the very same thing[9]. Gawande described how he learnt to establish the patient's priorities rather than impose the medical approach. Whereas he had previously done most of the talking, bombarding the patient with facts and figures, now he asks the patient to talk about his goals, his unacceptable outcomes and how he understands his situation. Above all Gawande learnt to listen as the patient told his story – all of his story – no longer asserting control by speaking. He listened supportively but dispassionately, accepting what is said without colluding or colliding.

Summary

The ability to listen is, like salt, crucial to the maintenance and preservation of humanity and God's creation. The nature of that listening requires the listener to be comfortable with her own spiritual journey and be able to listen with her whole being. This type of listening has no agenda but accepts the person where they are, regardless of belief. The listener lays her beliefs on one side in order to be a supportive presence that neither colludes nor collides with the other person's faith, belief or world view. The listener has no need to speak as she does not seek to control but rather to enable the person to identify and connect with his own beliefs. In contrast society's attitude to listening is somewhat ambivalent – listening does not produce anything or make a profit and generally its effects are not visible. There is no obvious measurable outcome from time spent listening so the medical approach is to focus on solving the problem rather than on the patient. Even when we focus on the other person we may find ourselves talking to avoid listening because we are not comfortable with what we hear. When we listen 'in full colour' rather than 'in black and white' we may become aware of their suffering, spoken or unspoken.

1 Treasure ,J. (2011) 'Five Ways to Listen Better',
www.ted.com/talks/julian_treasure_5_ways_to_listen_better
2 Guenther, M. (1992) Holy Listening, London: Darton, Longman & Todd: 148.
3 Long, A. (1990) Listening, London: Darton, Longman & Todd: 48
4 Ralston, H. (2014) Personal communication (Extract from unpublished thesis).
5 Beatty, J. (1999) 'Good Listening', Educational Theory Vol 49(3): 281–298.
6 Corradi Fiumara, G. (1990) The Other Side of Language (A Philosophy of Listening), London: Routledge: 30.
7 Vest, N.(1994) No Moment Too Small, Cambridge, Massachusetts: Cowley Publications: 21.
8 Rankin, M. (2007) in du Boulay, S. Cicely Saunders The Founder of the Modern Hospice Movement, (expanded ed) London: SPCK: 193.
9 Gawande, A. (2014) The Reith Lectures: The Future of Medicine BBC Radio Four.

Food for thought

- Do I recognize the difference between listening in black and white and listening in colour?
- Do I listen at a deeper level?
- Do I accept that speaking is a way of asserting control?
- Do I speak to assert control?
- Do I speak to avoid hearing what the other is saying?
- Do clergy and church leaders speak to assert control?
- Does the church/do clergy/leaders listen for the inner pain of members of the congregation? Do they believe there is anything to be heard?
- Is the church/are clergy/leaders comfortable or uncomfortable with suffering? What are the signs of this comfort/discomfort?

Chapter eight
Staying with the pain

Introduction

We have explored spirituality as a concept and examined our own spirituality through various exercises and reflections. We also saw the importance of listening as a way of valuing the person – but when we listen we risk hearing something painful. We need to be able to identify, acknowledge and process our own pain if we are to be able to stay with the pain of others. The exercises in the earlier chapter on spirituality will help us identify our own pain and our personal experience of processing pain will help us to help others. In this chapter we shall consider our possible responses to the suffering of others. Illustrations and examples from my own experience and that of other hospice chaplains are offered to help negotiate this topic, which of itself may be painful.

Recognizing and owning my pain

Whatever the nature of our role it is easy for us to distance ourselves from and even forget our deep experiences of the Holy Spirit working in us. Anyone in a leadership role may benefit from asking themselves whether, as Henri Nouwen argues, they have become used to 'running the show as a circus director'[1]. Nouwen argues that familiarity with his own inner life is essential for any minister in order to recognize and name his own experience, and then be able to use it to help others. I am saying that familiarity with your inner life is essential for any Christian, not just leaders, who feels led to help other people. That help may be listening without speaking but it may also be speaking the unspeakable when the other person is struggling to find the words to express the pain of the experience. At this point you may find it helpful to retrieve and revisit the lifeline exercise undertaken earlier. Give yourself time to reflect on whether any of your painful experiences have informed or influenced your response to another's pain.

Response to the suffering of others

Few people will acknowledge the gift of being able to stay with those who are in a place of pain, a place where they are vulnerable and broken. However if we believe that God suffers with creation for the sake of its completion we too can respond to suffering with compassion. For most people their spontaneous response to suffering is either to flee or fix it by finding a quick cure. Neither of these responses stays with the person in their place of pain. They are both examples of numbness, ways of avoiding suffering, not seeing and not wanting to see, trying to protect the self against sharing the suffering, possibly through busyness and material goods. Neither of these responses shows the action of salt, rather numbness suggests that salt is not present.

The opposite of this numb reaction is agony – agony caused by engaging with the suffering, as Jesus the divine engaged as a man with human suffering. Agony is choosing voluntarily to walk alongside the suffering person, to feel with them but not like them – although some have entered and shared the pain of the other. We speak of rubbing salt in the wound – it is painful just as it is painful to engage with the suffering of others.

The German theologian Dorothee Soelle observed: '"Numbness" is a metaphor for apathy, "agony" a metaphor for compassion'[2]. If we are affluent, reasonably well off or even just comfortably off it is easy for us to assume that we are doing things right, that we are on God's side and God is on our side. We become insensitive to the sufferings of those who are struggling, those in difficult circumstances, and it does not occur to us that God might be on their side suffering with them. We might even think that the sufferers are betraying God, not realizing that we have assumed that God maintains the status quo of society – necessary if we are to avoid facing the unpalatable truth that we are the oppressors or the cause of the suffering. Our comfortable lives are an anaesthetic which produces apathy, enabling us to avoid acknowledging the existence of the suffering. Without such an acknowledgement we cannot recognize that such suffering is a sign of injustice. Without such an acknowledgement we cannot recognize that we have lost our saltiness. Rather than acknowledge God's suffering and the people's suffering, the apathetic salt-free society depersonalizes and objectifies prisoners, workers, patients, by giving them numbers or naming them by their crime, job or affliction.

At this point we need to check our understanding of Christ's suffering. Do I believe that Jesus really suffered or do I, perhaps subconsciously, believe that his divinity somehow protected him? Alternatively do I believe that Jesus's suffering was all that needed to be done? My suffering then becomes irrelevant to this suffering-free salvation. The desire to want to be in God's image without being in Christ's image betrays a lack of understanding of the nature of salvation and a need for instant and easy gratification. Such a salvation has no place for the pain expressed in the primal scream – a spontaneous and unrestrained scream, not necessarily audible, expressed as a result of recalling a particularly disturbing past experience usually from early in life. The scream may express, for example, repressed anger, frustration, despair, desperation, isolation, confusion… Not only does a suffering-free salvation ignore emotional pain but it also excludes the recognition and transformation of spiritual pain.

Just as Jesus did not escape from the pain so we too are called to stay with the pain, 'sharing Christ's suffering' (1Peter 4:13). By God's grace we resist the temptation to escape into apathy or numbness. We are called to see as God sees and to share God's suffering through the death of Jesus. Like God we are powerless. Whatever adjective is used: powerless, empty, lonely, it is the Gethsemane element in compassion:

> To watch with Jesus, not to fall asleep during the time of his fear of death, which lasts till the end of the world and has in view all the fearful, is an ancient Christian demand that is contrary to every natural response to affliction[3].

Recognizing when that natural response is likely to assert itself is important. Just as the disciples in Gethsemane lost their sense of the nearness of God and fled to the numbness of sleep so we too need to recognize when physical and emotional exhaustion may lead to numbness or apathy and thus losing our saltiness. A friend who worked as a hospice chaplain recognized that the numbness of physical and emotional exhaustion brought him 'close to cracking up'. He spoke with his line manager who arranged some immediate leave for him and amended the frequency of his clinical supervision so that he could return to being salt.

Response to the pain of the other

When we recognize the pain of another person, whether by hearing their primal scream or seeing their body language, we know that for them to move on they need to be able to put their pain into words. However, that may not always be possible or appropriate. There are times when 'we must learn the practice of listening to silences'[4]. Are we prepared, like the hospice chaplain, to see Christ in all we meet? The chaplain sees Christ in the patient and connects the patient's feeling of alienation to Jesus's alienation on the cross. The chaplain also believes that God is ever-present and, regardless of whether the patient has faith, her prayerful presence links the patient's wounds to those of Christ. The chaplain does not offer advice but stays with the pain. We too need to be present as people 'who can tolerate not-knowing, not-curing, not-healing and face with us the reality of our powerlessness'[5].

One hospice chaplain, sitting with a patient who was in a coma, described being conscious of something happening … but there were no words to describe it. This same chaplain described his personal conviction that there are no definitive answers and spoke of the frustration he feels when anyone tries to close or limit an experience to an explanation. His body language was such that it felt like horror rather than frustration and I asked if he was like the character in Munch's painting The Scream – he answered 'yes'. I did not ask whether he was screaming on behalf of the patient or screaming his own frustration. Either way the point is made that the scream – even when it is silent, even when there is no indicative body language – is an aspect of the spiritual journey which needs to be heard and acknowledged. When I hear my own scream I am able to articulate it using biblical words of grief and lament but nowadays few people have any kind of knowledge of the language of liturgy and prayer. These words have to be offered to the person, spoken simply and directly, so that they can say 'Amen'. Even when the person has some knowledge of the Bible and/or prayer there will almost certainly still be a need to explain the use of the language to enable them to speak from the heart, expressing their own feelings. However, there may be people whose incapacity or illness prevents the spoken expression of their suffering and there will be those who share their story but without verbalising the suffering.

On some occasions when I 'heard' the patient's scream I expressed the suffering in poetic form or in prayer, depending on my understanding of the patient's beliefs. Invariably this was met with tears – a nonverbal form of expression. The text box gives an example of a prayer-poem written for a man whose brain tumour was reducing his ability to communicate. It is based on what little information was gleaned by the nurses and me. If you are an Anglican you will realize that I have used a loose version of the

Collect for Purity, often used as the Prayer of Preparation at the beginning of Communion services, as the framework for the first part of this piece.

Almighty God,
I don't know if you're real
I've seen no sign of your presence.
You may have created the world
But my wife destroyed my world by walking away.
They say all hearts are open to you
Well you've made me feel vulnerable and worthless
They say all desires are known to you
But there was no desiring
Only rejection and the absence of love
And they say no secrets are hidden from you
But there were secrets – every family has them
I know I'm not perfect but I did my best for them
And now they won't visit so I cannot say 'sorry'.
I long for their love, my wife's especially
And there's nothing I can do
I'm shattered and filled with despair

But if you are real
If you are there
Please help her to know
That I care.
Before I move on
I need peace of mind
Don't let it be long – please be kind –
the tumour is changing me
Give me peace whilst I still have my mind.

When I read it to him the man cried. Thus it was possible to facilitate the expression of the suffering, but the difficulty in the secular hospice setting was finding or adapting the words to avoid (being accused of) proselytization.

The hospice chaplain's role of enabling the patient to recognize and express suffering occurs against the backdrop of our society's attitude to death, dying, bereavement and mourning. Despite the efforts of the Dying Matters Coalition, to help people talk more openly about dying, death, bereavement and plans for the end of life, these are still not mainstream topics of conversation and neither are they accepted as part of everybody's everyday life. Discussions on end of life care and euthanasia are still needed as cases of the administration of excess morphine continue to make the news headlines. Where death and related topics are still taboo the role of the chaplain is counter-cultural but to what extent has the church colluded with the taboo? Collusion that avoids pain suggests a loss of saltiness. To what extent do Christians collude and why?

If we as a society wish to value what it is to be human per se – without reference to cognitive or physical ability, without reference to independence or contribution – it is necessary to be honest about our feelings. To be salt we need to speak of anger and revenge transformed by redemption and forgiveness and of that sense of the transcendent which so often surprises us. The academic definition of spirituality suggests that it may not be only words that take us beyond ourselves to the sense of the transcendent:

> a generic characteristic of human beings that reveals itself in
> the search for meaning, relationships, purpose and hope[6].

For some it is music, for others art, family relationships, pets, a hobby or sport. The difficulty lies in recognizing that these things can all be a source of spiritual nourishment and a doorway to our sense of the transcendent.

Summary

The natural response to the suffering of another is either to flee or to fix it. Many people respond emotionally, sometimes with tears, but still they flee. Even those whose response is to donate to an appropriate charity are avoiding the issue, they are apathetic and numb to the pain, without salt. To stay with the pain is to be salt staying with the agony, out of which may rise a prayer like 'Lord have mercy' or the groaning of the Spirit helping us in our weakness: 'we do not know how to pray as we ought, but that very Spirit intercedes with sighs too deep for words' (Romans 8:26).

1 Nouwen, H. (2014) *The Wounded Healer*, (new ed) London: Darton, Longman & Todd (first published 1979).

2 Soelle, D. (2001) *The Silent Cry*, Minneapolis: Fortress Press.

3 Soelle, D. (1975) *Suffering*, Philadelphia: Fortress Press.

4 Swinton, J. (2007) *Raging with compassion*, Cambridge: Eerdmanns Publishing Company: 101.

5 Swinton, J. (2007) *Raging with compassion*, Cambridge: Eerdmanns Publishing Company: 101. 6 Holloway, M., Adamson, S., McSherry, W., and Swinton, J. (2010) *Spiritual Care at the End of Life, a systematic review of the literature*, London: Department of Health.

Food for thought

• *What is your response to the suffering of others? Do you flee? Do you want to find a quick cure? Do you recognize that you can do nothing but stay with the person anyway?*

• *How do you help the person to express their suffering? If there are no words are their feelings denied or can they be expressed another way? If so how? Do you use the words of the Psalms?*

• *How does your church respond to the suffering of others? Are disasters and tragedies included in intercessory prayers?*

• *To what extent has the church colluded with the taboo on death and dying? To what extent do Christians collude and why?*

Chapter nine

No pain – no gain

Introduction

Travelling across London to visit my parents in the late 1970s the sight of men living on the streets upset me. My husband was distressed by my tears but neither of us knew what to do with those tears. Fifteen years later I was leading a mother and toddler group where the mothers found themselves upset by the television news pictures of starving children. In those intervening years I had learnt to pass my distress, my pain, my emotions, to God in prayer: 'Lord, have mercy'. I did not ignore or deny my distress but held it and handed it over. I explained this to the mothers – some of them later told me that they had taught their children to say 'Lord have mercy' when they saw distressing news.

This principle of handing pain to God is valid for all kinds of pain, whatever the cause. During my early years in healthcare chaplaincy I slowly learnt that the more I identified and handed over my own pain – from memories of past hurts, painful experience of present attitudes, awareness of wrongs not owned, and all that is entailed in failing to love my neighbour as myself (Mark 12:30–31) – the less emotion was involved in my caring. Rather than being emotional my caring was compassionate. The more I identified and handed over my own pain the less obstructions there were in my relationship with God and in my relationships with those to whom I ministered.

Accepting the other: the carer's pain as the source of care

When I consider the transformation that takes place from Good Friday to Easter Sunday I am surprised that the transformation of a negative event into sustaining energy is rarely recognized and articulated. After all the cross stands at the centre of the Christian faith – a cross holding the crucified body of Jesus and an empty cross signifying his resurrection. The crucifixion shows the reality of God's suffering because 'God so loved the world that he gave his only Son, so that everyone who believes in him may not perish but may have eternal life' (John 3:16). This incomprehensible love freely accepts suffering and leads disciples to likewise follow the way of passion, thus 'completing what is lacking in Christ's afflictions' (Colossians 1:24). This does not mean that Jesus's death was not sufficient but rather that his death has made it possible for us to become who God made us to be, made in God's image, and to share in the redemption of all creation:

> For the creation waits with eager longing for the revealing of the children of God … and will be set free from its bondage to decay and will obtain the freedom of the glory of the children of God. (Romans 8:19&21)

Or as Jean Vanier expressed it:

> That is why Jesus had to leave this world.
> He had to go
> so that we could become Jesus,
> continuing his work[1].

Christ's crucifixion and resurrection had to happen for Christ to be ever-present in the world: 'And remember, I am with you always, to the end of the age' (Matthew 28:20b). Without his suffering there would be no presence of which we could be a part. Without his suffering we would not experience God sharing our suffering. Christ's suffering was transformed ånd we too need not only to own and offer our suffering for transformation but to take up our cross for the redemption of creation. We cannot become God's image without Christ

– there is no pain-free way. Many Christians have experienced tragedy – death of a child or relative, suicide of a relative, divorce, serious illness, redundancy, collapse of a major project – but how many have offered that tragedy to God for transformation? How many have made the connection between the transformation of personal pain and the ability to minister and walk alongside others? Just as salt has to be dissolved to bring out the flavour of food or to preserve food so we too have to be transformed. By the power of the Holy Spirit our pain can be dissolved or transformed to be used as the means of caring for God's creation and ensuring that all creation flourishes.

If Christians are indeed concerned to be whatever the other person needs then concern with their own spiritual journey and their own relationship with God is to be expected, as is self-examination for that which might obstruct that relationship. Such obstructions might be memories of past hurts, painful experience of present attitudes, awareness of wrongs not owned, and all that is entailed in failing to love my neighbour as myself (Mark 12:30–31). The point is that whatever the source of the wound or suffering it can be transformed by God. As poet Richard Shannon wrote:

> Wounded oysters build out of gory wounds a pearl.
>
> And create within the gap of pain a jewel.
>
> May we be so wise[2].

Without the grit there would be no pearl: 'Then he began to teach them that the Son of Man must undergo great suffering, and be rejected' (Mark 8: 31). I was disappointed that of the twenty-five hospice chaplains I interviewed only one spontaneously spoke of the transformation of his personal pain into a creative force which sustained him and enabled him to support others in dealing with their pain. Other interviewees recognized that personal incidents had influenced them but did not spontaneously make the link with transformation into sustaining energy for their work. Another way of looking at this was expressed by Henri Nouwen when he criticised the church hierarchy for thinking that 'man can be led out of the desert by someone who has never been there'[3]. Pope Francis expressed similar concern when he asked priests to be shepherds living with the smell of the sheep. Fortunately we have a gracious and generous God who fills the gaps, supplies the salt when necessary so that, despite the absence of transformed pain, the other person feels accepted and receives love and care.

Accepting the other: making space for them

The immediate benefit of the transformation of pain is the space that is created when the pain is released. If I am to minister to another, I must make room for them. However, the nature of the transformation is such that not only does space increase but unconditional love and compassion grow too. There is more room for God and more room for others. The self that is 'full of itself' cannot receive the other, nor make a genuine movement toward the other[4]. The self has to make room for the other. One of the chaplains I interviewed spoke of the need for space in himself in order to be able to reflect with another human being: 'if I'm full-up with my own unreflected stuff there's no space to be the witness'. Another spoke of 'not getting in God's way' and another frequently used the word 'conduit', to convey that she is a channel for the transmission of God's love. This does not mean thinking less of oneself in the sense of putting oneself down but as Paul says thinking of oneself with sober judgement (Romans 12:3) and therefore thinking of myself less, thus making room for the other.

If we think of a pastoral encounter like the meeting of chaplain and patient, or like you meeting someone for 'coffee and a chat', as an embrace we see that it needs to be mutual[5]. If one party is stronger than the other this strength may be perceived as power and domination, thus destroying mutuality. Just as salt is used to bring out but not destroy the flavour of food so salty Christians enable the other person to feel valued rather than belittled. Boundaries are needed so that a sense of self is preserved for both parties. The identity of both is preserved and yet both are transformed by the relationship. Neither seeks to absorb the other, and neither seeks to understand the other, for a claim to understanding again slips into a power-play. Each has to see the other as an other for the embrace to be genuine and mutual. One chaplain spoke of allowing patients to see and explore at their own pace – which he admitted could be frustrating. However all human beings have a basic personal need for self-worth, security and significance.

The ability of the chaplain, or any carer, to see the other as other may be limited or marred by her own need for self-worth, security and significance[6]. Should the chaplain or any personal carer, consciously or unconsciously, view the embrace or the person being embraced as fulfilling those needs the embrace is no longer mutual and is not genuine. Not only is the chaplain's need likely to clog the channel but it may take from the other, causing diminishment, or it may create a false self which will also block the channel. Rooted in God/Christ the essence of significance, security and self-worth is transformed. As concepts they are empty of substance but in Christ they are creatively full and free to give birth to the true God-given self.

A chaplain who had only been in post for a short time described the process of having to let go of an identity rooted in doing and then finding and accepting an identity rooted in being. It was a steep learning curve for he had come from a strongly mission-oriented congregation. He conveyed a sense of spiritual struggle to hold in tension the task depicted in Jesus's Great Commission (Matthew 28:19) and the requirement of his job, to be present with folk in a way that encouraged them to explore their own perception of spirituality. Letting go of an identity rooted in doing, and finding and accepting an identity rooted in being-in-Christ is a necessary process for discovering who God made us to be, how to be salt and how to practice embodied care.

Embodied care

Rooted in Christ I am comfortable with myself and my spiritual journey, the bad times as well as the good, the pain and the tragedy as well as the joy and the celebration. Only then am I able to support another without colluding or colliding. When I support or accompany another I do so with all of me: 'the greatest asset which any of us offers to another in caring relationships is ourselves, the self we have reflected upon'[7]. This is what is meant by 'embodied' care and in my experience it describes what is offered by hospice chaplains. Whilst there are few hospice chaplains who are not wounded healers the interviews I conducted revealed that recognition of the transformation of their own suffering was rare. Such transformation is not readily spoken of even by hospice chaplains. For many people this is still a difficult or grey area. The British 'stiff upper lip' has not encouraged self-reflection or the expression of pain, but it is this pain, these wounds that can be the source of healing. It is my own experience of pain and tragedy, redeemed and transformed, which enables me to be sensitive to pain in others and to stay with them as they try to come to terms with circumstances or make peace with self, family and, possibly, God. This has been described as a boundary area, of which one of my chaplaincy friends said:

> We stand in places where others fear to go, alongside the Medicine men who occupy the boundaries between health and illness and the Shamans who hold boundaries between life and death. As Our Lord found, demons live in deserts because kings occupy the defined boundary land[8].

To stand in this limbo-like place is to stand in the gap for the other person, for creation, just as Christ stood and stands in the gap for us.

No matter what our job or role is or how skilled we are these are not the means of or the reason for standing in the gap. Neither will they make us the salt so desperately needed by creation. Being salt is to have an identity rooted in Christ. Being salt arises from knowing who I am in Jesus.

Summary
Pain consumes energy and spiritual pain is no exception but acknowledging Jesus in the pain opens the door to transformation. The negative effect of the pain is transformed into positive energy which for the hospice chaplain fuels the ability to care. Release from pain also creates space for the other but the carer needs to be constantly alert to the balance of the relationship, ensuring mutual respect. Thus the carer's own experience of pain is the source, through transformation, of the care offered to others. All human beings have a basic personal need for self-worth, security and significance. Society today tends to view work and possessions as supplying these needs whereas Christians understand God, Father, Son and Holy Spirit as the way by which those needs are fulfilled. Therefore Christians themselves need to be examples of that fulfilment, knowing who they are in Jesus and being the salt of the earth that will preserve and care for humanity.

1 Vanier, J. (1988) *The Broken Body*, London: Darton, Longman & Todd: 68.

2 Quoted in Campbell, A. (1986) *Rediscovering Pastoral Care*, (2nd ed), London: Darton, Longman & Todd: 37.

3 Nouwen, H. (2014) *The Wounded Healer*, (new ed), London: Darton, Longman & Todd (first published 1979).

4 Volf, M. (1994) *Exclusion & Embrace*, Nashville, TN: Abingdon Press: 141

5 Volf, M.(1994) *Exclusion & Embrace*, Nashville, TN: Abingdon Press: 143

6 Crabb, L. (1977) *Effective Biblical Counselling*, London: Marshall Pickering: 56– 57

7 Kelly, E. (2012) *Personhood & Presence*, London: Continuum: 5.

8 Blake, L. (2002) 'Chaplains living on the Boundaries' *Association of Hospice & Palliative Care Chaplains Newsletter* (Summer edition, 2002).

Food for thought

- *When are you most likely to react sentimentally or with emotion?*
- *How do you 'complete what is lacking in Christ's afflictions' (Colossians 1:24)?*
- *Think of ways in which your spirituality has benefitted from the transformation of personal pain.*
- *Think of ways in which your ministry has benefitted from the transformation of personal pain.*
- *Do you think that without the transformation of pain there would be no ministry?*
- *Reflect on your pastoral relationships to assess whether they are mutual. Do any of them fulfil your needs?*
- *Does your church hierarchy think that suffering is a necessary experience for leaders?*
- *Explore the similarities and contradictions between Jesus's Great Commission (Matthew 28:19) and encouraging people in their own perception of God.*

Chapter ten

Being salty today

Introduction

Salt was once so rare that it was considered valuable and the salt trade routes were protected by Roman soldiers. It is even reputed to have been used as currency. Indeed it is said that in parts of Ethiopia it is still used as currency. Today salt is far from rare and more likely to be considered dangerous than valuable. We are concerned to manage our salt intake because too high an intake can cause raised blood pressure which can increase the risk of heart disease and stroke. So the reputation of salt has declined from valuable to dangerous. Is the same true of Christianity? Like salt Christianity was once valued and the Church and its ministers were respected. In parts of the world Christianity is still valued and respected providing the backbone of society, but in our society attitudes are often ambivalent and even antagonistic. Many non-Christians think that Christians are alienated from contemporary society, yet many Christians suspect that non-Christians are alienated from what it is to be human. To not only survive but to flourish humanity needs the relationship with God. Christians, being like salt, are the means by which that relationship can be restored. However, becoming salt is an on-going process of acknowledgement that Jesus's statement 'you are the salt of the earth' applies to us as much as it did to the disciples all those years ago. In the becoming we learn about ourselves, our identity in Christ, and the society in which we live. Becoming salt is a work-in-progress with the ultimate goal of the flourishing and the preservation of God's creation.

This is not something to be undertaken lightly nor by oneself. Salvation in Christ is indeed personal but the development of identity takes place in community.

Identity and community

Unfortunately our society has become immune to the value of community – where once neighbours looked out for each other today many people do not know their neighbours and even those who do are often too busy to look out for them. Without the habit of neighbourly concern, now often labelled as nosiness, loneliness and isolation flourish. Community also played a part in the upbringing of children but where the texture of community became threadbare disaster struck, as illustrated in the Bulger case in 1993 when two ten-year-old children forgot who they were, or perhaps never understood what it is to be human, and murdered a two-year-old. More recently we have the case of the sixteen-year-old boy who raped and murdered a six-year-old girl on the Isle of Bute – because he 'just wanted the life experience'. More recently still a seventeen-year-old girl was knifed to death seemingly caught in drug turf-wars, because she was in the wrong place at the wrong time. It appears that in all three cases the perpetrators had no moral yardstick to guide them, no sense of belonging or living by society's values. They had no sense of being a person whose identity conformed to society's external expectations. They acted with impunity, and if they conformed to anything it was to a behaviour code which says that anything goes, including murder.

Currently there is major concern about children being coerced into gangs, often drug-related. In order to survive these children have to conform to the gang's values. These are insidious external expectations which force the children to become something they were not. They have to create a false self which distorts their identity and does nothing to nurture their humanity. Just as the presence of salt in a casserole brings out the flavour of the food might the presence of a Christian, who is prepared to be there without criticising or commenting, bring out something of the child's original undistorted identity?

Identity and external expectations

You may not personally have experienced the external expectations described earlier, of institutional Christianity or of paternalism, but over a third of the population grew up in a society in which what other people thought was really important. When I first started in hospital chaplaincy over twenty years ago I met a patient, a ninety-year-old lady, whose friend told me that they went to church together. I asked whether they would like to receive communion together in the ward. The ninety-year-old patient replied firmly that she would not as her mother would definitely not approve!

The external expectations derived from Christianity may have been swept away but this has not left a vacuum. Many people, particularly millenials and generation Z, have filled the gap with expectations derived from Twitter, Instagram, bloggers and influencers. Millenials, those born between the early eighties and the millenium grew up as the internet became widespread. They adapted rapidly to social media and constant connectivity. Generation Z, those born since the millennium, never knew a time without such technology – they take it as a given. Social media provide a variety of attitudes and behaviours from which the individual may consciously choose to form their identity. However, it is arguable that these expectations are rarely consciously chosen and are more likely to be unconsciously absorbed. Either way the expectations are not promulgated by any external community but held consciously or unconsciously by the individual and their effect is real, limiting or distorting the development of identity. For an individual to flourish they need to develop socially, emotionally, mentally and spiritually.

Spirituality

Our society socializes and educates us in such a way that objective knowledge, like facts and information, is more important than subjective knowledge learnt through the senses, both outer and inner. We find our subjective knowledge, our intuition, dismissed, deemed of no value and so we ignore it and ultimately lose the ability to exercise it. In this way we become immune to that which can nourish and sustain us as human beings. For some this leads to mental illness whilst others lose or fail to develop their sense of what it is to be human. Some will become suspicious of and antagonistic to community.

However, there are signs that attitudes are changing. Several of the hospice chaplains I interviewed for my research observed that they had recorded in patients' notes events of spiritual significance such as 'watching the swans' and 'enjoying an ice-cream'. None of the other staff queried these entries. Rather, such comments can open the door for others to express similar experiences. Furthermore, newspapers and magazines now feature articles openly concerned with spirituality – usually generic rather than in connection with any particular faith or belief system. There have also been many articles espousing the benefits of walking in the countryside, being active, having a hobby and taking care of oneself. Concern for the natural world has also made the headlines and more people are taking notice. Christians as salt may find themselves in situations where they can speak of what a sunset, the night sky, playing or listening to music, a cycle ride or running a marathon does for them. Equally likely are situations where speaking is not appropriate, neither the Bible nor faith are mentioned. As salt the Christian simply has to be there with the person. In both cases the Christian will probably need to reframe their understanding of what it is to preach the gospel.

Being salt and preaching the gospel

Given that Jesus's instruction: 'Go into all the world and preach the gospel to all creation' (Mark 16:15) is referred to as the Great Commission some will find the idea of preaching as silent presence difficult. Laying spoken evangelism to one side and replacing it with the quiet and inconspicuous evangelism of presence may not be easy. St Francis is reputed to have instructed his followers to spread the gospel but to use words only when necessary. Yet God can and does work through our willingness to be with another person. We are not apparently offering anything, doing anything, not even speaking, but God is at work. It is like the Jewish concept of 'sitting shiva' – simply sitting with someone who is grieving. The focus is on their need, not mine, and I pray for the humility not to think less of myself but to think of myself less and the other person more.

If you are wondering how we can be salt and 'make disciples' I suggest that the difficulty lies with our understanding of the instruction 'make disciples'. Do we tend to think of making disciples as being like making a cake or making a bookcase or making a model… is our understanding that we are to do something? Are we 'converting'? In other words we are the subject and the other person is the object. Or the church is the subject and the nations or the people of the nations are the object. Are we guilty of thinking that we, the church of God, have a mission when it is the God of mission who has a church? It is possible that having searched and worked on our own attitudes to others – whether we regard them as subject or object – we are then able to facilitate reflection on the attitude of the Christian community/church/chapel to which we belong. By God's grace we may be the salt that changes and transforms the flavour of that particular community.

Christian identity

Christian identity does not come from external expectations. It is not dependent on gifts or talents, nor on anything you do or own. It is not dependent on any relationship other than the relationship with God: Father, Son and Holy Spirit. Christian identity is modelled on the identity demonstrated by Jesus when he says 'I do not look to men for honour' (John 5: 41 Revised English Bible). Understanding honour as validation Jesus is saying that his identity is not grounded in other people. His identity is grounded in God and he further expresses his confidence in his grounded identity: 'Even if I testify on my own behalf, my testimony is valid, for I know where I came from and where I am going' (John 8:14).

Learning who I am in Christ, becoming more Christ-like, is a work-in-progress. This transformation is how we become salt and even whilst we are in the process of becoming we demonstrate through our way of being, our behaviour, that we are disciples of Christ, the salt of the earth. Just as salt appears to be inert yet has a major effect on food in flavour and preservation so Christians may appear to be inert by not speaking of God but conveying God's love by their presence. As salt Christians value the other person rather than focusing on themselves. They are aware of their own motives and needs and ensure that these are put on one side so that they may listen in colour, staying with the pain of the other person. However, Christians know that self-care, addressing the motives and needs with a spiritual director or soul-friend, is necessary for the maintenance of their saltiness. They know that self-care is not selfish, neither is it sinful, for just as salt needs to be stored in dry conditions to stay free-flowing so Christians need conditions of self-care to stay present in society and be the means by which God's people flourish and God's creation is cared for.

The contemporary context

In this contemporary context we must ask ourselves whether our society today seeks to manage or control Christians lest they raise awareness of issues like poverty and justice and cause the status quo to be disrupted.

Where once Christian values were embedded, were even the foundation of our culture, it is no longer so and values and integrity are often hard to find. Care and consideration for others is now replaced by a sense of entitlement regardless of the damage it does to other people. Lives are lived at such a pace that it seems likely that few have reflected on this and so the demise of care and the rise of entitlement have occurred unnoticed. The result is an unconscious sense of entitlement which encourages an equally unconscious feeling of impunity, or at the very least the unacknowledged sense of entitlement does nothing to develop a conscious sense of personal responsibility for right and wrong. Newspapers abound with examples like the cyclist who was prevented from going through a red light by a pedestrian legitimately crossing the road. The cyclist jumped off his bike and punched the pedestrian who was badly hurt, needing to go to hospital. Consider your own experience of having a driver pull out in front of you without even looking or the driver who forces you to give way when actually the parked cars are on their side of the road and technically it is your right of way.

Entitlement is a twenty-first century sin which has crept up on us. In a world where the concept of sin is itself often deemed irrelevant entitlement seems acceptable. However, I am not suggesting that Christians should criticize or judge. Rather we should realize that entitlement is a sign of emptiness, something to fill a hole, counteract restlessness, give a sense of purpose and value. Christians know that only God can fill that hole, calm the restlessness, give a sense of purpose and value and God does this through us. Just as only salt can preserve and bring out the flavour so we are God's salt through whom creation will be preserved and humanity will flourish.

I'll end with a reminder of my definition of Christians as salt:
We, 'the salt of the earth' also known as disciples of Christ, are an essential nutrient for all creation, the earth and humanity. We cannot become salt by ourselves, nor can we be made salt by any other aspect of creation. We play a vital role in the regulation of activities which

are society's bodily functions. We are to be found in all walks of life.

Our presence is essential for organisations to work properly and fairly, and be accountable for their business practices and their treatment of employees.

Our presence is essential to ensure that society's attitudes to all people, including the poor, the disadvantaged, the sick, the unemployed, the homeless, refugees, prisoners, are influenced and guided by justice and mercy expressed in loving care and concern.

Our presence is essential to ensure that society's attitudes to our environment in creation are not dulled by greed, expediency or apathy.

In short we Christians are essential for the maintenance of a balanced, just and fair society – where we are missing, low in numbers or have little influence a culture of entitlement and even impunity may develop and society become lawless.

My hope is that Christians will not only explore how they can be salt but realize that our society needs the salt of Christianity.

Appendix

Two Guided Meditations

Each biblical passage is printed out twice, the second time with comments and questions to guide your meditation printed in italics.

Moses and the burning bush

Moses was looking after the flock of Jethro, his father-in-law, priest of Midian. He led his flock to the far side of the wilderness and came to Horeb, the mountain of God. There the angel of Yahweh appeared to him in the shape of a flame of fire, coming from the middle of a bush. Moses looked : there was the bush blazing but it was not being burnt up. 'I must go and look at this strange sight,' Moses said 'and see why the bush is not burnt.' Now Yahweh saw him go forward to look, and God called to him from the middle of the bush. 'Moses, Moses!' he said. 'Here I am' he answered. 'Come no nearer' he said. 'Take off your shoes, for the place on which you stand is holy ground. I am the God of your father,' he said 'the God of Abraham, the God of Isaac and the God of Jacob.' At this Moses covered his face, afraid to look at God. Exodus 3:1–6

Ask the Holy Spirit to use my imagination so that I am in Moses' place. Picture the scene – the shrubby landscape, the heat, the sheep searching for grass.

Moses was looking after the flock of Jethro, his father-in-law, priest of Midian.

Picture Moses – what is he wearing? As Moses what am I wearing? Is the flock large or small? Are there lambs as well as adult ewes? Am I looking after sheep? Or am I looking after people/children/things?

He led his flock to the far side of the wilderness and came to Horeb, the mountain of God.

What is the wilderness landscape like? What is Moses thinking and feeling/ what am I thinking and feeling?

and came to Horeb, the mountain of God.

What is the landscape like now? What is Moses thinking and feeling as he approaches the mountain of God? Am I approaching God? What am I thinking and feeling?

There the angel of Yahweh appeared to him in the shape of a flame of fire, coming from the middle of a bush.

What is Moses' initial reaction? What is my first thought? What do I feel?

Moses looked : there was the bush blazing but it was not being burnt up. 'I must go and look at this strange sight,' Moses said 'and see why the bush is not burnt.'

Is this just curiosity? If not what is the motivation?

Now Yahweh saw him go forward to look, and God called to him from the middle of the bush. 'Moses, Moses!' he said. How does Moses react when his name is called? What does it take for him to answer? Do I hear my name called?

'Here I am' he answered. How do I answer?

'Come no nearer' he said. 'Take off your shoes, for the place on which you stand is holy ground. I am the God of your father,' he said 'the God of Abraham, the God of Isaac and the God of Jacob.' What does Moses feel now? How do I feel about taking off my shoes?

At this Moses covered his face, afraid to look at God.

How do I react? Am I afraid?

Close with a prayer

Jesus appears to Mary Magdalene

[11] Now Mary stood outside the tomb crying. As she wept, she bent over to look into the tomb [12] and saw two angels in white, seated where Jesus' body had been, one at the head and the other at the foot.

[13] They asked her, 'Woman, why are you crying?'

'They have taken my Lord away,' she said, 'and I don't know where they have put him.' [14] At this, she turned around and saw Jesus standing there, but she did not realize that it was Jesus.

[15] He asked her, 'Woman, why are you crying? Who is it you are looking for?' Thinking he was the gardener, she said, 'Sir, if you have carried him away, tell me where you have put him, and I will get him.'

[16] Jesus said to her, 'Mary.' She turned toward him and cried out in Aramaic, 'Rabboni!' (which means 'Teacher'). [17] Jesus said, 'Do not hold on to me, for I have not yet ascended to the Father. Go instead to my brothers and tell them, "I am ascending to my Father and your Father, to my God and your God."'

[18] Mary Magdalene went to the disciples with the news: 'I have seen the Lord!' And she told them that he had said these things to her. John 20:11–18

Ask the Holy Spirit to use my imagination so that I am in Mary's place. Picture the scene, the garden, the tomb…

[11] Now Mary stood outside the tomb crying. As she wept, she bent over to look into the tomb [12] and saw two angels in white, seated where Jesus' body had been, one at the head and the other at the foot. *What did Mary expect to see? What do I expect to see?*

[13] They asked her, 'Woman, why are you crying?' *How do I feel about angels?*

'They have taken my Lord away,' she said, 'and I don't know where they have put him.' *What is Mary feeling? What do I feel?*

[14] At this, she turned around and saw Jesus standing there, but she did

not realize that it was Jesus. *What is Mary feeling now? What do I feel now?*

[15] He asked her, 'Woman, why are you crying? Who is it you are looking for?'

Thinking he was the gardener, she said, 'Sir, if you have carried him away, tell me where you have put him, and I will get him.'

16 Jesus said to her, 'Mary.' *What effect does this have on Mary? Do I hear Jesus say my name? How do I feel?*

She turned toward him and cried out in Aramaic, 'Rabboni!' (which means 'Teacher').

17 Jesus said, 'Do not hold on to me, for I have not yet ascended to the Father. Go instead to my brothers and tell them, "I am ascending to my Father and your Father, to my God and your God."' *Does Mary understand what she is being asked to do? What is Jesus asking me to do?*

18 Mary Magdalene went to the disciples with the news: 'I have seen the Lord!' And she told them that he had said these things to her.

Close with a prayer